PRUNING
TECHNIQUES

Alison R. Francis

TIME
LIFE
BOOKS

Alexandria, Virginia

TIME®
LIFE
BOOKS

Time-Life Books is a division of Time Life Inc.
Time-Life is a trademark of Time-Warner Inc and
affiliated companies.

Time-Life Inc.
Chairman and Chief Executive Officer Jim Nelson
President and Chief Operating Officer Steven Janas

Time Life Books
President Larry Jellen
Vice President and Publisher Neil S. Levin
Vice President, Content Development Jennifer L. Pearce
Senior Sales Director Richard J. Vreeland
Director, Marketing and Publicity Inger Forland
Director of Trade Sales Dana Hobson
Director of Custom Publishing John Lalor
Director of Rights and Licensing Olga Vezeris
Director of New Product Development Carolyn M. Clark
Executive Editor Linda Bellamy
Director of Design Kate L. McConnell
Project Editor Paula York-Soderlund
Design Assistant Jody Billert

Originated in Singapore by Master Image.
Printed and bound in China by Excel Printing
10 9 8 7 6 5 4 3 2 1

School and Library distribution by Time-Life
Education, P.O. Box 85026, Richmond, Virginia
23285-5026.

Library of Congress Cataloging-in-Publication Data
Francis, Alison, 1957-
   Pruning techiques / Alison R. Francis.
   p. cm.-- (Time-Life garden factfile)
   ISBN 0-7370-0634-X (spiral bound)
   1. Pruning. I. Title. II. Series.
SB125 .F678 2001
631.5'42--dc21   00-051185

For PAGEOne
Creative Director Bob Gordon
Editors Alison Copland, Jane Simmonds
Art Editor Tim Stansfield
Picture Research Louise Thomas
Commissioned Photography Peter Anderson
Illustrations Karen Gavin

For Marshall Editions
Managing Editor Anne Yelland
Managing Art Editor Helen Spencer
Editorial Director Ellen Dupont
Art Director Dave Goodman
Production Nikki Ingram, Anna Pauletti
Editorial Coordinators Ros Highstead, Gillian
Thompson

Note: Measurements are given in imperial and in
metric (in parentheses) and should not be
interchanged.

CONTENTS

Introduction   5

THE WHY, WHEN, AND
HOW OF PRUNING

Why prune?   8
When to prune   12
How to prune   16
Tools for the job   18
Pruning terms   20

SHRUBS AND TREES

Pruning shrubs   24
Shrub categories   26
Shrubs in containers   32
Wall-trained shrubs   34
Pruning hedges   36
Pruning trees   40

ROSES

Pruning roses   46
Rose categories   48
Routine rose care   54

CLIMBING PLANTS

Pruning climbers   58
Supporting plants   62
Popular climbers   64

FRUIT TREES AND BUSHES

Pruning fruit   72
Apple and pear trees   74
Other fruit trees   82
Soft fruit   88
Grapevines   92
Thinning fruit   94

SPECIAL PROJECTS

Training plants   96
Bonsai   102
Feature plants   104
Houseplants   106
Kitchen crops   110

Index and acknowledgments 112

INTRODUCTION

O f all the gardening practices, pruning is the one that fills many gardeners with dread. This book aims to show you that it is not that complicated and that incorrect pruning is rarely, if ever, terminal. The worst that can happen is that maybe the plant will not flower for a season, or bear as many fruits.

PRUNING BASICS

Pruning is carried out for many reasons and the why, when, and how are discussed in the opening chapter of this book, followed by a checklist of what needs pruning and when.

The three degrees of pruning – hard, moderate, and light – are explained, along with the importance of shaping, basic pruning principles, and how to make the right pruning cut.

Tools are important. A pair of sharp pruning shears is probably the tool you will use most, while loppers will take care of thicker stems. A pruning saw will be useful for cutting heavy or thick branches, and a pair of heavy-duty gloves are a must. The best tools for the job and caring for them are looked at in more detail. There is also a glossary of some of the most commonly used pruning terms.

INDIVIDUAL NEEDS

Many shrubs thrive without any routine annual pruning, but they will produce a better show of flowers and fruits if given some attention, even if it is just removing dead and damaged shoots. In this book, shrubs are divided into six main categories, each with specific pruning requirements, which are then looked at in more detail. Roses are another group of plants that have special pruning needs. Each category of rose is covered, together with the most appropriate method of pruning.

CLIMBING PLANTS

With their different growing habits, climbing plants have their own pruning needs. It is important to choose the right kind of plant for a particular structure, be it trellis, screen, arch, or pergola.
The plant will need the correct initial pruning to train new growth around the support.

Pruning established climbers and taming neglected ones are examined, while a handy checklist looks at what climbers need pruning, when to prune them, and how.

PRUNING FRUIT

The reasons for pruning fruit trees and bushes are the same for any other tree or shrub. New plants need to be trained for health, shape, and productivity; once established, the plants need regular maintenance pruning to remove dead, diseased, and badly placed branches and shoots. Fruit trees and bushes also need pruning to encourage a good harvest and to allow light and air to reach the ripening wood so that it can grow strong enough to carry the load.

Soft fruit are less demanding when it comes to pruning, the easiest being cane fruit – raspberries, blackberries, and hybrid berries – while currants and blueberries need an annual pruning routine if they are to remain productive.

SPECIAL PROJECTS

Training plants into decorative shapes involves pruning not so much for the health of the plant but more for our enjoyment of it.
The art of topiary and the special pruning requirements needed to fashion geometric or fantasy shapes out of living plant material are reviewed in this book.
Also covered are the hard pruning of both topgrowth and roots necessary to form bonsai. Other techniques include pinch pruning, stopping growth, curbing highfliers, and cutting a rubber plant down to size.
Armed with the pruning information and advice given in this book, together with a sharp pair of pruning shears and heavy-duty gloves, you will be equipped to tame any wild growth, and produce healthier, stronger plants with better flowering and fruiting.

The why, when, and how of pruning

Why prune? 8
Looks at the many good reasons why you should prune your garden plants

When to prune 12
Describes how to decide on the optimum time to prune different types of plant

How to prune 16
Examines the different types of pruning, and describes how to make the right cuts

Tools for the job 18
Explains choosing and using the correct tools for all your pruning tasks

Pruning terms 20
Demystifies pruning by explaining clearly the most common terms you will come across

THE WHY, WHEN, AND HOW OF PRUNING

When left to their own devices, plants such as shrubs and trees, roses and climbers, fruit trees and berry bushes, and even houseplants and greenhouse tomatoes, will all grow, as long as they have adequate water, light, heat, and food. By giving them some assistance in the form of pruning, however, you can help them to grow better and stay healthier and, in consequence, they will reward your efforts by flowering and fruiting more prolifically.

This chapter looks first at the reasons behind why pruning is necessary for the well-being of certain cultivated plants, and the best times to take up the pruning shears and tackle the job. It then covers topics such as how much of the plant to remove at any one time and how to select the correct tools for the job. At the end of the chapter, there is a useful glossary of all the common words and phrases used throughout this book.

WHY PRUNE?

Some inexperienced gardeners may find pruning a puzzling and complex task. Put simply, pruning is the cutting back of unwanted shoots, stems, or branches of woody plants, such as shrubs, trees, and roses. It serves both to curb any straggly overgrowth of the plant and also to stimulate the production of fresh, new growth. This creates a well-shaped specimen that is strong and healthy, with improved flowering or fruiting capabilities.

REASONS TO PRUNE

■ **Encouraging growth** Pruning is only strictly necessary when something begins to go wrong with a plant. There are several reasons for needing to cut back a shrub or tree. For example, if it starts to outgrow its allotted space in the garden; if it becomes straggly and untidy; or if flowering or fruiting starts to decline. Removing old wood encourages the production of new shoots which, in turn, will flower and fruit more prolifically. The harder you prune the more vigorous the new growth. This is the basic principle that lies behind why most pruning is carried out.

■ **Staying healthy** If a plant starts to die back, cut out any dead or diseased shoots to promote fresh, healthy growth, giving the plant a new lease on life.

■ **Increasing fruit yields** Fruiting plants need a more structured annual pruning routine if they are to produce optimum yields. In this case, pruning is a preventative measure rather than a cure. For successful crops, remove old wood regularly to ensure the constant production of new and vigorous flowering and fruiting shoots.

REVERTED SHOOTS
Variegated-foliage plants such as *Euonymus fortunei* sometimes produce shoots with all-green leaves. Remove any of these as soon as you see them, using sharp pruning shears.

UNWANTED GROWTH

- **Retaining color** If a variegated plant "reverts," meaning that it produces shoots with all-green leaves, swiftly remove any rogue shoots to restore order. Reverted shoots should be pruned out as soon as they occur, otherwise they will take over the plant. These shoots have a higher chlorophyll content than variegated shoots and are more vigorous.

- **Suckers** These unwanted growths often appear around the base of trees and roses; always remove them as soon as you spot them.

- **Water or epicormic shoots** These fast-growing shoots sometimes arise from dormant buds or near pruning cuts on tree trunks. They proliferate quickly and sap energy from the tree. Remove them immediately by cutting them right back to their point of origin, otherwise they will deprive healthy new growth of valuable nutrients.

RECOGNIZING ROSE SUCKERS
Rose suckers arise from a plant's base and bear leaves that have a different appearance than those on the rest of the plant.

IMPROVING SHAPE
AND CONDITION
You can quickly
improve the shape
and health of a
mature tree or
shrub, such as this
flowering quince, by
taking out any
shoots or branches
that look either dead
or diseased, or that
are crowding or
crossing over each
other. This will allow
light and air into
the center.

SHAPING AND TRAINING

Another reason for pruning is to improve the existing shape of a tree or shrub. To do this, you need to remove healthy but unwanted wood as well as unhealthy growth. Cut out all dead, dying, congested, and crossing shoots and branches. This will allow light and air to enter and circulate the plant, helping it to produce new, strong, healthy growth in a neat and balanced shape.

Fruit trees are often trained to make the most of limited space or to open them out. By removing crossing and crowded branches, air and light are allowed in to ripen the fruit on lower branches. Ornamental and fruit trees can be trained in decorative shapes (see p. 74), such as espaliers, or fanned out against walls. On fruit trees, branches are often trained horizontally for ease of harvesting.

SIX GOOD REASONS FOR PRUNING	
• To improve the condition of the plant, by removing unhealthy branches.	• To control size or restore the stability of an overgrown plant.
• To stimulate growth, by letting light and air into the center of the plant.	• To improve or change the shape of a plant, such as in pleaching or topiary.
• To encourage more prolific flowering and cropping.	• To create special effects, such as colored winter stems (see p. 31).

■ **Special pruning** Topiary and bonsai are special pruning methods used for training shrubs and trees to a specific shape or purpose. This "creative" pruning is a little more complicated and calls for patience and a steady hand but, as with all pruning, the results can be immensely satisfying. Other decorative features that demand careful pruning include creating a laburnum arch, a rose swag, or a standard plant.

Exactly where and how much to prune depends on the health of the individual plant and what you want it to look like in future years. Both timing and technique depend on the age and type of plant. Pruning will inevitably cause the plant some stress, so always have a clear idea of exactly what you are trying to achieve before you start to cut.

SHAPED IVY
This variegated 'Gold Heart' ivy has been trained on a support and shaped with pruning to create an eye-catching feature for the patio.

WHEN TO PRUNE

The timing of pruning is crucial and depends on the growth habit of the plant. Most flowering shrubs, including roses, produce flower buds either on new growth or on wood that is just one year old, and it is this that determines the best time to prune them. Deciduous trees are best pruned when they are dormant during winter, but evergreens should be left until the weather warms up.

TYPES OF PLANT

■ **Flowering shrubs** For the vast majority of flowering shrubs, and especially those that bloom in spring and early to midsummer, the ideal time to prune is immediately after the flowers have finished their display. This will give the plant plenty of time to produce strong new flowering stems for the following year.

For shrubs that flower in late summer and fall, it is better to delay pruning until the following spring, rather than cutting back the plant straight after flowering. Pruning late in the season will encourage tender, young shoots to grow, leaving them exposed and likely to succumb to frost damage over the winter months.

■ **Fruiting plants** For both edible and ornamental types of fruiting plant, pruning is usually carried out during the fall or winter months after fruiting has been completed. However, some of these plants will also need attention during the summer months.

■ **Deciduous trees** These should be pruned from late fall until late winter, when they are not producing any new growth. With the arrival of warmer weather in spring, strong new growth will be encouraged and any wounds will quickly heal.

CONTROLLING PLANT GROWTH
If a plant's stems are spilling onto a lawn making it difficult to mow or if it is crowding out other plants in a bed, you may need to cut it back, even when it is in flower.

Warning

Never prune in frosty or cold weather or during hot, dry spells, when plants are more vulnerable to disease and damage. The cooler and damper months of fall and spring are much more suitable for pruning.

■ **Evergreens** It is best to prune evergreen shrubs and trees in spring, after all danger of frost has passed. They may also benefit from a light trim after flowering to tidy up the stems that have flowered.

■ **New plants** When planting out, it is a good idea to tidy up the topgrowth and roots of pot-ready and bare-rooted plants.

Prune out any broken or torn branches and roots, making clean cuts. Untangle the roots of bare-rooted plants and spread them out in the planting hole, cutting off any that are twisted or very long.

A RIOT OF ROSES
The rewards of good pruning are clearly visible in this delightful rose garden. The plants are all strong and healthy, and flowering profusely.

CONTROLLING GROWTH

In addition to the basic pruning carried out to improve shape and stimulate new growth, shrubs, climbers, and roses also need cutting back regularly. For example, access along paths may become difficult or even hazardous if the plant in question has thorns or prickly leaves. These plants may also encroach on space needed by other plants or spill onto a lawn. In the growing season and spring, you may need to perform basic cutting back, as well as tying in, once a month in order to regain control. Some tidying up may also be needed in spring to repair any winter damage.

AFTER PRUNING

Pruning can be a bit of a shock to a plant's system. The plant also has to work harder to produce new growth. After spring and summer pruning, it is best to water the plant thoroughly and apply the appropriate fertilizer. Take time to weed around the plant too, then add a layer of mulch. For plants that were pruned in winter, do not feed or water them until spring, when they start back into growth after dormancy.

LAVENDER HEDGE
This lovely hedge is at its prime, and provides the perfect example of a plant that should be trimmed back only when flowering has finished.

A QUICK GUIDE TO PRUNING TASKS

TIME	SUBJECT OR TASK
Early to midspring	Late summer- and fall-flowering shrubs. Shrubs with colorful stems. Gray-leaved shrubs. Bush, shrub, climbing, and standard roses. Clematis (except early flowering kinds) and wisteria. Cut back dogwoods (Cornus) for winter stems.
Late spring	Spring-flowering shrubs, such as forsythia and the flowering currants (Ribes), as their blooms fade. Reshape evergreen shrubs if necessary. Thin and cut back any unwanted growth. Check fan-trained fruit and remove any unwanted shoots.
Early summer	Look for signs of silver-leaf disease on stone fruits, such as plums, cherries, peaches, and apricots, and cut away any infected branches.
Midsummer	Late spring- and early summer-flowering shrubs, such as broom (Cytisus) and lilac (Syringa), as blooms fade. Stone fruit, such as cherries and plums. Espalier- and cordon-trained fruit trees. Lightly prune vigorous large-flowered (hybrid tea) roses and wisteria.

A QUICK GUIDE TO PRUNING TASKS

TIME	SUBJECT OR TASK
Late summer	Clip evergreen hedges, such as box and yew, and trim topiary to shape. Trim lavender hedges after flowering.
Early fall	Prune rambling roses.
Late fall	Lightly prune roses to reduce the possibility of damage caused by wind-rock.
Winter	Cut back and trim beech *(Fagus)*, hawthorn *(Crataegus)*, and privet *(Ligustrum)* hedges. Prune deciduous trees and shrubs to improve their shape and maintain balanced growth.
Midwinter	Finish pruning apple and pear trees. Cut back stems of newly planted bush fruits. Halve the lead shoots of gooseberries and red and white currant bushes. Cut back black currant bushes.

YEW

HOW TO PRUNE

Cutting techniques and methods vary according to the type of pruning being carried out. It is very important that you use the correct one for the plant and style that you have chosen, otherwise the plant may suffer. If in doubt, it is better to err on the side of caution.

DEGREES OF PRUNING

There are, in general, three degrees of pruning: hard (or severe), moderate, and light. Hard pruning encourages vigorous growth, while a light prune slows down the rate of growth.

■ **Hard pruning** This involves removing a large amount of new growth from all over a plant or cutting a few shoots back hard where more growth is desired. When hard pruned, existing growth is cut back by at least three-quarters or down to about three or four buds from the base.

■ **Moderate pruning** This style of pruning results in about half the amount of any new growth on a plant being reduced by around half of its length. Cutting is spread evenly over the entire plant.

■ **Light pruning** A light prune cuts down about one-quarter of any new growth by no more than one-quarter of its length. In some cases, just the the tip of each shoot, about 2–3in (5–7.5cm) is removed. As in the case of moderate pruning, the pruning is spread across the whole plant.

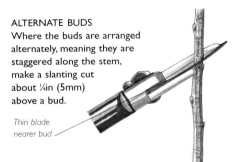

ALTERNATE BUDS
Where the buds are arranged alternately, meaning they are staggered along the stem, make a slanting cut about ¼in (5mm) above a bud.

Thin blade nearer bud

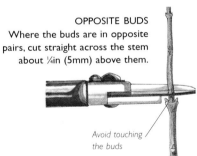

OPPOSITE BUDS
Where the buds are in opposite pairs, cut straight across the stem about ¼in (5mm) above them.

Avoid touching the buds

CREATING A WELL-BALANCED SHAPE

• When pruning any shrub, tree, or rose, try to imitate the plant's natural growth habit.

• Avoid overdrastic pruning: be sympathetic to the natural size and shape of a plant, and give it the amount of space it deserves.

• In order to encourage well-balanced and symmetrical growth, cut back any strong shoots lightly, and cut back weaker ones heavily.

• If strong shoots are cut back very hard, leaving too much weak growth, the plant will not flourish.

PRINCIPLES OF PRUNING

■ **Removing unhealthy growth** Aim to remove all dead, damaged, and diseased wood and weak, straggly, or misshapen growth. Always cut back to healthy wood. Cut away and burn dead and diseased wood before the problem spreads through the plant. Straggly growth is unsightly and saps a plant's energy.

■ **Creating an open framework** Cut back some of the main stems to the base. An overcrowded plant will suffer, so prune it back sufficiently to allow air and sunshine to reach the ripening wood and swelling buds. Remove any suckers, as well as branches that are crossing or rubbing against others.

■ **Making a clean cut** Always tidy up any jagged edges or tears to prevent disease entering the wound.

■ **Collecting up all prunings** Soft and healthy wood may be composted, but burn or otherwise dispose of any woody or diseased prunings.

■ **Feeding and mulching** After pruning, apply a generous handful of general fertilizer around the base of the plant, then apply a good mulch of leaf compost, shredded bark, or wood chips to retain soil moisture and suppress weeds.

■ **The golden rule** Too little pruning is always better than too much.

MAKING THE RIGHT CUT

All pruning cuts should be as small, clean, and neat as possible, which is why it is so important to have the right tools (see p. 18). Prune before shoots become too woody and before twigs become branches because young wood heals faster.

■ **Slanting or straight?** When cutting between buds arranged alternately on a stem, always make a slanting cut, to let water roll off the cut surface. When cutting above a pair of healthy opposite buds, make a straight cut, taking care not to damage the buds.

■ **Where to cut** If you cut too far from a bud, the wood left above it will wither and become susceptible to disease. If you cut too close to a bud, you risk damaging the bud itself. Never cut just beneath a bud, and avoid snagging or tearing the bark. Always prune just above a bud or a leaf, and new shoots will then sprout from just below the cut.

COLORFUL WINTER STEMS
Cutting this dogwood (*Cornus alba* 'Sibirica') back hard in spring produces these attractively colored young stems the following winter.

TOOLS FOR THE JOB

Having the right tools for each garden task is of vital importance, and this is especially true when it comes to pruning. Always buy the best-quality tools you can afford and make sure they stay sharp. Pruning tools include various shears, saws, knives, and loppers.

WHAT YOU NEED

■ **Loppers** A pair of pruning loppers or long-handled pruning shears is useful for removing thick branches and old, hard wood. The longer the handles the longer the reach and the more leverage you will have, meaning you will have to exert less effort. Loppers will tackle wood up to ¾in (2cm) thick. For tall-growing shrubs and climbers, a pole pruner with extendable arms is a good investment.

■ **Sharp pruning shears** Pruning shears must always be sharp: blunt blades will tear or crush the stem, which can lead to dieback or allow infection to set in. This is particularly important when pruning roses.

There are two types of cutting blade: single (anvil) and double-bladed (bypass or scissor). The single-bladed model has one sharp, hard metal blade, which cuts through with a biting action to a softer metal anvil. The double-bladed model works with a scissorlike action, in that the two blades bypass each other.

A good pair of pruning shears can be used to prune all soft stems as well as woody ones up to ½in (1cm) in diameter. Brightly colored handles make it easier to find the tool if you put it down somewhere, and make sure it is fitted with a safety catch to keep the blades closed when not in use.

■ **Chain saw** Always wear protective clothing when using this tool, and handle it with extreme care. Consider using a chain saw if you have branches more than 4in (10cm) thick to tackle. Rather than buy one, borrow a chain saw from a local tool-rental company. Alternatively, use a professional tree surgeon, but obtain an estimate for the work beforehand.

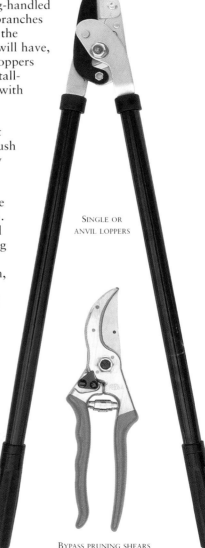

SINGLE OR
ANVIL LOPPERS

BYPASS PRUNING SHEARS

■ **Shears** Hand or hedging shears need to be kept sharp and oiled. They are useful for trimming hedges and general tidying. Crinkle-edged blades cut through thick shoots more easily, but are difficult to sharpen.

■ **Powered hedge trimmer** An electric hedge trimmer makes light work of trimming a hedge, although hand shears are better for a short hedge or for trimming individual shrubs. The longer the cutting length, the quicker you will cut the hedge. The more teeth there are on the blade, the finer the finish, although wide-spaced teeth will cope better with thicker shoots. Make sure there is a protective hand shield on the machine, a lockoff switch to prevent accidental starting, and a ground-fault circuit interrupter (GFCI) on the electrical supply.

■ **A pruning knife** This needs a keen edge to clean up any jagged pruning cuts, but take great care not to cut your fingers. After use, wipe the blade dry and rub it with an oily cloth after use.

PRUNING SAW

■ **Pruning saw** Use a bow or other narrow-bladed pruning saw for thick wood. Unlike a carpenter's saw, a pruning saw has wide-set, splayed teeth, that are less likely to get clogged up when cutting through live, green wood.

■ **Gardening gloves** A pair of heavy-duty gardening gloves, preferably leather, is essential to protect your hands from sharp blades and prickly stems or foliage.

■ **Shredder** Use this to reduce trimmings in bulk before composting.

CARE OF PRUNING TOOLS

• Store all tools in a dry place to prevent rusting.

• After use and before putting them away, clean and dry tools thoroughly.

• Oil all the moving parts from time to time.

• Keep tools sharp. Either sharpen them yourself or take them to a specialist at least once a year.

• Never leave your tools lying around outside.

PRUNING TERMS

There is a whole new vocabulary for you to learn when it comes to pruning. Most of it is just common sense and you will soon become familiar with the terms. Use this glossary regularly to remind yourself of precise meanings as you read through the rest of the book.

GLOSSARY

ALTERNATE BUDS
Buds that grow singly at different heights and on different sides of a stem.

ANGLED CUT
The cut used when pruning stems that have alternate buds (compare "Straight cut"). Make a slanting cut just above and sloping away from the bud.

BRANCH COLLAR
A thickened ring of tissue at the base of a branch.

BUD
A swelling on a plant stem containing an embryonic leaf or flower. A growth bud produces either leaves or a shoot, and a fruit bud produces flowers, which are followed by fruit.

CALLUS
The scar tissue that forms over a pruning cut.

COPPICING
Regular pruning back of shrubs or trees close to ground level to stimulate the growth of vigorous new stems.

CORDON
A method of training a tree (either an ornamental or, more usually, a fruiting tree) to produce a single, upright stem with no large side branches.

DEADHEADING
The removal of spent flowers from flowering shrubs to stimulate further flowering. It prevents seed production at the expense of plant growth and the formation of the following season's buds.

DIEBACK
Death of shoot tips, usually caused by damage such as frost or disease.

ESPALIER
A method of pruning and training fruit trees to grow flat against a wall, fence, or other support.

FAN
A method used for growing fruit trees, such as cherries, up against a wall or fence. Branches of a young tree are encouraged to grow up in a fan shape from as close to the base as possible, supported by wires and ties to keep them in place.

CALLUS OR SCAR TISSUE

GLOSSARY

FEATHERED MAIDEN
A one-year-old tree that has developed lateral shoots, which are known as "feathers."

FRUIT BUD
On a fruit tree, a bud that produces flowers and fruit rather than foliage or a shoot. A fruit bud is larger and rounder than a growth bud.

FRUIT SPUR
A growth from a branch or three-year-old sideshoot.

GRAFT UNION
The point on the stem of a shrub, tree, rose, or woody climber where the topgrowth has been grafted onto the rootstock, resembling a ring of callus.

GROWTH BUD
On a fruit tree, a bud that produces foliage or a shoot rather than fruit.

LATERAL
A side growth arising from a root or shoot.

LATERAL BUD
A bud that will form a sideshoot.

LEADING STEM OR LEADER
All trees and some shrubs produce a main or central stem, or trunk, from which all the side branches develop. Growth can be controlled by cutting the leader out.

MAIDEN
A tree that is in its first year of growth.

PINCHING OUT (OR STOPPING)
The removal of the shoot tip or bud to encourage sideshoots to form and to restrict growth.

PLEACHING
The training of deciduous (sometimes flowering) trees on a post-and-wire framework, so that their branches entwine to form a green wall or hedge, or overhead canopy, such as a laburnum or wisteria arch.

POLLARDING
Severe pruning of tree branches at regular intervals in order to promote the growth of more young shoots, thereby preventing the tree from reaching its natural size and form.

PLEACHED LIME TREES

GLOSSARY

RENEWAL PRUNING
A method of pruning by which the plant is cut back really hard, removing older growth in favor of younger shoots, to give it a new lease on life.

ROOT PRUNING
Trimming the roots of a plant before planting or replanting it. When you buy a bare-rooted plant, as opposed to a container-grown one, you may need to trim the roots to make planting easier. This is usually the case with bare-rooted roses. Trim back roots to 9in (23cm), and also remove any dead, diseased, or damaged ones. Root pruning is also carried out on established trees and shrubs. For example, a fruit tree such as a plum that produces lots of leafy growth and very little fruit may have an overdeveloped root system. When the plant is dormant, dig a trench around the tree or shrub 2–5ft (0.6–1.5m) away from the main stem. Cut through any thick roots that are uncovered.

ROOTSTOCK
A plant used to provide a root system for the topgrowth of another plant (scion) that is grafted on. This method is commonly used for roses.

SIDESHOOT
A shoot growing outward from a stem.

SPUR
A short shoot or branchlet on fruit trees, bearing flower buds then fruits.

STANDARD
A tree or trained shrub with a single straight stem devoid of branches.

STRAIGHT CUT
The cut used when pruning stems with opposite buds (compare "Angled cut").

SUBLATERAL
Sideshoot from a lateral shoot.

SUCKER
A shoot arising from below ground level, some distance from the plant, or growing from the rootstock of grafted plants.

TIP PRUNING (OR TIPPING BACK)
Pinching or cutting out shoot tips to encourage sideshoots to develop or to remove damaged growth.

VEGETATIVE GROWTH
Nonflowering, usually leafy growth.

WATER (EPICORMIC) SHOOTS
Unwanted, fast-growing, sappy shoots, usually arising from the site of damage or pruning cuts.

WEEPING
A shrub or tree with a pendulous habit, either natural or induced.

WEEPING STANDARD
This tree has been trained as a weeping standard. It has a single stem crowned with a head of pendulous branches.

SHRUBS AND TREES

To give their best, ornamental shrubs need
some degree of pruning throughout their
lifetime, and this chapter starts by looking
at the individual pruning requirements of
the main shrub categories: early- and
late-flowering shrubs, evergreens and gray-
leaved shrubs, ones with colorful stems,
and small-leaved types. A quick guide to
some of the most popular garden shrubs
gives advice on when and how to prune
them. The needs of shrubs grown in
containers, wall-trained shrubs, and
hedges, are also covered in detail.

Most trees need little pruning once
established, but formative pruning in
the early years will lay the basis of a
well-shaped and healthy mature tree.
Among the subjects covered here are
when to prune, the safe removal of
branches, removing suckers, root
pruning, pollarding and
pleaching, pruning
conifers, and how
to deal with
overhanging trees.

PRUNING SHRUBS

O rnamental shrubs generally grow and flower without any help, and most require little or no pruning other than the removal of dead or diseased shoots. In some cases, however, it becomes necessary to use the pruning shears – to encourage better flowering or to keep the plant within bounds, controlling the height, shape, or thickness of growth. Left alone, shrubs keep growing upward and outward, with any flowers appearing higher and higher on the plant each year.

2

ORNAMENTAL SHRUBS

Whatever the shrub, there are several important points to bear in mind when pruning.

■ **Shape and balance** The purpose of pruning is to form a shapely shrub with strong, young branches that are well-spaced to allow light and air into the center.

■ **Cutting cleanly** You should always use sharp tools to make a clean cut, either close above a healthy bud, slanting away from it or, if removing a branch or sideshoot, flush with the main stem. Any jagged edges and crushed stems should be trimmed neatly with a sharp knife.

■ **Unwanted growth** Aim to take out all dead and diseased wood, crossing or rubbing branches, and any weak and spindly shoots. Depending on the individual plant, remove stems at ground level, either to an outward-facing bud or to sound, green wood.

■ **Treating pruning wounds** In the past, it was recommended that all cuts of more than 1in (2.5cm) across should be treated with a wood sealant or fungicide in order to prevent disease entering the plant. This course of action is no longer considered necessary; it may, in fact, do more harm than good.

FLOWERS OR FOLIAGE?
If unpruned, the smoke bush
(Cotinus coggygria) bears lots
of flowers; if pruned in spring
it will produce more leaves
for bright fall color.

SHRUB-PRUNING CHECKLIST

BERBERIS
Thin out old wood after flowering in spring. Clip hedges after flowering.

BUDDLEIA
Cut back *B. davidii* in early spring to within 4 or more buds of the base. Shorten shoots of others after flowering.

CALLUNA
Trim off old flower spikes in early spring.

CAMELLIA
Cut back leggy mature plants after flowers fade.

CEANOTHUS
Prune spring-flowering types grown against a wall to within 2 buds of the previous season's growth after flowering. Thin freestanding plants in spring, also removing dead wood. Cut back summer-flowering types to 2–6 buds in spring.

CHAENOMELES
After flowering, take out old wood and thin and shorten sideshoots.

CHOISYA
Cut out any old wood and prune to shape in spring if necessary.

COTINUS
Trim in early spring if you want more foliage.

COTONEASTER
Hard prune old bushes in spring.

CYTISUS
Perform an annual tidy-up after flowering, but take care not to cut beyond the previous year's wood.

ELAEAGNUS
If necessary, thin and shape in spring.

ERICA
Trim the plant with hand shears to remove dead flowers and retain shape.

ESCALLONIA
Thin and prune wall-trained plants to maintain shape as flowers fade.

FORSYTHIA
If growing against a wall or fence, remove old flowering shoots after flowers fade. Thin freestanding shrubs every 3–4 years.

FUCHSIA
Remove any dead growth from small plants in spring. Large (hardy) types do not usually need pruning.

GARRYA
Prune after flowering, if necessary, to retain shape.

JASMINE
Hard prune winter jasmine after flowering. Thin out summer jasmine after the flowers have faded.

PHILADELPHUS
After flowering, take out old flowering shoots and thin the rest. Give older plants a new lease on life

by pruning them back hard in spring.

PIERIS
Prune after flowering in late spring.

RHODODENDRON
Rejuvenate old bushes by hard pruning in spring; otherwise remove dead flower heads.

RIBES
Older bushes benefit from a hard spring prune.

SPIREA
Remove old flowering shoots of spring-flowering types after flowering. Hard prune late summer-flowering types in early spring.

WEIGELA
Remove any leggy shoots after flowering.

2

LAUREL
(*LAURUS*)

SEP 19 01

SHRUB CATEGORIES

It is vital to know when a shrub will be in bloom, because taking the shears to a flowering shrub at the wrong time will probably mean few or no flowers during the following season. For pruning purposes, shrubs divide into six main categories: early-flowering shrubs; late-flowering shrubs; foliage evergreens; flowering evergreens and gray-leaved shrubs; shrubs with colorful stems; and small-leaved shrubs.

2

EARLY-FLOWERING SHRUBS

Shrubs such as forsythia and flowering currants *(Ribes)* produce their flower buds on what is called "old wood," or stems grown in the previous year. These shrubs must be pruned as soon as flowering is over in order to keep them in check and to encourage better flowering next year. In general, they require little more than a thorough tidy-up.

Remove some of the older flowering branches, which have hardened brown or gray bark, and branches that have no visible growth buds. Thin any overcrowded, crossing branches, but try to retain as much as possible of the new, flexible, green growth, because this will carry the following year's flowers.

Some of these woody shrubs can become straggly and misshapen as they mature. You can hard prune these, taking all dead wood, as well as a few of the older, larger stems, back to ground level (see below). At the same time, prune younger flowering stems back to about half of their original length, to just above a point where some new growth (a strong sideshoot) is emerging.

PRUNING FORSYTHIA
TO NEW SHOOT

Prune older shoots back to where strong new growth emerges

HARD PRUNING FORSYTHIA
With more mature shrubs, as well as pruning back to new growth, remove dead wood and some of the older woody stems at the base.

■ **Broom** Common broom *(Cytisus scoparius)* and hybrids like *Cytisus × praecox* 'Allgold' will become leggy if not pruned annually. After the plant has flowered, clip it with hand shears to remove flowering shoots, cutting back to buds close to the main stems. Avoid cutting old wood, as this may kill the plant.

■ **Exceptions to the rule** Tall-growing shrubs, such as lilac *(Syringa)* and viburnum, need thinning only every three or four years, removing old, weak, and diseased stems and any others to maintain the shape. With fruiting shrubs, such as cotoneaster, lightly trim the flowering branches, leaving flowers to develop into berries.

Strong, healthy, new growth appears soon after pruning

EFFECT OF CUTTING BACK A VIBURNUM

2

SHRUBS TO BE PRUNED DIRECTLY AFTER FLOWERING

Buddleia alternifolia
Chaenomeles (flowering quinces)
Corylopsis
Cytisus (broom)
Deutzia
Forsythia
Hamamelis
Jasminum nudiflorum

Kerria japonica
Philadelphus coronarius (mock orange)
Ribes (flowering currants)
Syringa (lilac)
Tamarix (spring-flowering)
Weigela

A MOCK ORANGE READY FOR PRUNING

LATE-FLOWERING SHRUBS

2

These shrubs produce flower buds on what is called "current season's growth," that is shoots produced earlier the same year. These shrubs should be pruned back hard as the weather warms up in early spring, giving the new wood plenty of time to develop its flower buds.

Cut back all the previous year's flowering stems to within two to four buds or shoots of the older wood. At the same time, cut out some of the older growth to prevent the shrub from becoming overcrowded. This will encourage new growth, which will flower later in the summer. If left unpruned, these shrubs tend to create a network of spindly twigs, while producing fewer and smaller flowers.

After pruning these late-flowering shrubs, it is a good idea to mulch around each plant with a 2-in (5-cm) layer of soil mix or well-rotted manure, together with a handful of a general fertilizer.

■ **Buddleias** The butterfly bush *(Buddleia davidii)* is a vigorous grower and its arching stems can be cut back even harder than other shrubs. Cut stems back to varying lengths to encourage flowering at different heights.

■ **Hydrangeas** These shrubs can be divided into three groups for pruning purposes. Established plants that flower on the current season's growth, such as *H. paniculata*, need to be taken back hard to a framework of branches near to the ground. Cut back the woody growth made in the previous season to one or two buds from the old wood. This degree of hard pruning will stimulate a display of larger flower heads.

SHRUBS THAT SHOULD BE PRUNED IN EARLY SPRING

Buddleia davidii (butterfly bush)

Caryopteris

Ceanothus (deciduous, not evergreen, types)

Fuchsia (hardy types, such as *F. magellanica*)

Hibiscus

Lavatera (tree mallow)

Leycesteria formosa

Spirea

Tamarix (summer-flowering types)

BUDDLEIA DAVIDII 'WHITE PROFUSION'

To help build up the framework of a young plant, leave some of the strong, new growth in the first couple of years, and just trim the main stems above a strong bud. In the third year, cut out half of the new growth.

Mophead and lacecap hydrangeas, such as *H. macrophylla*, flower on one-year-old wood. Old flower heads will give some protection to over-wintering flower buds, so delay pruning until the worst of the winter weather is over. Then prune back some of the old wood to the base and remove any weak shoots. Reduce all other stems by about 12in (30cm), cutting them down to a strong pair of buds.

Other species, such as *H. aspera*, require only minimal pruning to keep them tidy.

■ **Hardy fuchsias** As soon as hardy fuchsias start coming into bud in early spring, identify any dead stems and cut them away completely. At the same time, remove any weak or crowded stems and reduce all the remaining healthy wood by about one-third to leave one or two pairs of buds. Do not be tempted to prune any earlier, as winter rain could collect on the cut surfaces and rot the stems.

SPRING-PRUNED HYDRANGEA
This *Hydrangea paniculata* is starting to produce some strong flowering shoots for its summer display after pruning in early spring.

FOLIAGE EVERGREENS

The best time for pruning evergreen shrubs grown for their foliage is when the weather starts to warm up around midspring. They need little work other than the removal of dead growth. As they mature, however, they may become too large, or grow leggy and bare around the base. They will then benefit from hard spring pruning down to the young shoots at the base. This encourages tight new growth and a more bushy shape.

EVERGREEN AND GRAY-LEAVED SHRUBS

The following are some evergreen and gray-leaved shrubs that may need a light spring tidy-up:

Azaleas *(Rhododendron)*, *Callistemon* (bottlebrush), camellias (after flowering has finished), ceanothus (evergreen types), *Choisya ternata* (Mexican orange blossom), *Gaultheria* (pernettya), elaeagnus, escallonias (after flowering), garryas, *Helianthemum* (rock rose; after flowering has finished), *Ilex* (holly; these will respond to hard pruning if necessary), olearias, *Phlomis fruticosa* (Jerusalem sage), perovskias, photinias, pieris (remove frost-damaged shoots and deadhead plants), rhododendrons, and *Ulex* (gorse; after flowering has finished; old plants can also be pruned back severely).

FLOWERING EVERGREENS AND GRAY-LEAVED SHRUBS

With flowering evergreens and gray-leaved plants, delay pruning until after flowering. Deadhead and cut off long shoots in early fall. Prune overgrown plants back hard when the danger of frost has passed, but take care not to cut into old wood. It is a good idea to mulch around each plant with a 2-in (5-cm) layer of soil mix or well-rotted manure, and a handful of a general fertilizer, after pruning.

Unlike most evergreen shrubs, rosemary can be cut back hard to a low branch if it becomes overgrown and leggy. Do this after flowering and new shoots will soon appear from the old wood.

Regular pruning of gray-leaved shrubs such as cotton lavender *(Santolina chamaecyparissus)*, stops them from becoming leggy. Prune in spring as new growth begins. Dead topgrowth left over winter will protect new buds from frost and cold. Cut the plant back close to its base, where new shoots can be seen. These new shoots will soon grow.

REJUVENATING SHRUBS

Drastic action is called for when you are confronted with a mature shrub that has either grown very bushy with thin, flowerless stems, or has become extremely sparse and leggy.

You will need to be quite ruthless with the pruning shears, cutting the shrub down to within 12in (30cm) of the ground. Do this in spring as milder weather sets in, and after pruning be generous with water and give the shrub some proprietary fertilizer.

With luck, the plant will enjoy a fresh lease on life, sending out strong new shoots, which over the following few years can be pruned to produce an attractive plant once more.

If the plant dies, console yourself with the fact that at least you tried!

AVOIDING LEGGINESS
The gray-leaved cotton lavender *(Santolina chamaecyparissus)* responds to regular spring pruning by becoming bushy and flowering well.

COLORFUL STEMS

Some shrubs are grown mainly for their decorative winter stems; these include the dogwoods (*Cornus alba* and *C. stolonifera*), ornamental brambles *(Rubus cockburnianus)*, and some willows (*Salix alba* subsp. *vitellina* 'Britzensis' and *S. daphnoides*). Prune these back very hard at the end of each winter. This process is not carried out for the well-being of the plant but in order to stimulate the growth of numerous new and vigorous, brightly colored stems. It is a simple technique known as "coppicing" or "stooling."

Prune back the stems at the end of winter, before any new leaves have started to emerge. Using sharp pruning shears, cut back each stem to an outward-facing bud, about 2–3in (5–7.5cm) from the main stump of hard wood. Although this degree of pruning will look quite drastic initially, new growth in the form of young shoots will soon appear at the base. During the following winter your efforts will be amply rewarded by a display of vibrantly colored stems that will brighten up the dullest of days.

SMALL-LEAVED SHRUBS

Heathers (*Calluna*), heaths (*Erica*), and other types of small-leaved shrub are, in the main, used for creating ground cover. To keep them neat and compact, it is important that they receive an annual trim.

■ **All heathers** With age, these plants will become woody and leggy, and their flowering tends to deteriorate. You can prevent this from happening by cutting off spent flower spikes, using either a pair of sharp pruning shears or hand shears (which is probably the easier and quicker, if less accurate, way to do the job).

ROCK ROSES
Cistus is a flowering evergreen shrub that requires little pruning other than deadheading and removal of dead and diseased wood.

■ **Winter-flowering heathers** These should be pruned in spring, cutting close to the base of the previous year's growth, but not below the lowest healthy leaves. Do not cut into old wood as this could lead to the plant suffering dieback. Since these types are more compact, they may not need trimming every year.

■ **Summer-flowering heathers** The dead flower spikes can be left until early spring to protect the plant in winter, but if they are removed in the fall a bright flush of new growth will be your reward in spring.

■ **Tree heathers** These just need trimming after flowering to improve their appearance or shape.

2

SHRUBS IN CONTAINERS

The pruning requirements for shrubs grown in containers differ little from those grown in the open ground, but attention needs to be paid to watering and feeding a pot-grown shrub if it is to continue to produce healthy foliage and blooms. This is important if annual pruning is needed to keep the plant well-shaped. Root pruning may be necessary when you are repotting, particularly if the shrub is not going to be grown in a larger pot. It is best to carry out this operation in spring.

2

HANDLING LARGE POTS AND SHRUBS

There are several points to remember when you are dealing with large or heavy containers and large shrubs.

■ **Positioning the container** If you are transplanting a shrub into a heavy container, for example a large terra cotta urn or a concrete sink, place the container in its final position before starting to fill it with soil mix and planting it. Otherwise, you will find it too heavy to move afterward.

■ **Planting** Before transplanting a large shrub, water it well and prune it lightly into a well-balanced shape. Loosen the soil mix and always hold the shrub by a strong main stem if possible.

■ **Avoiding damage** Never hold the shrub by its young stems or leaves when moving it from pot to pot, since this is likely to cause damage from which the plant may not be able to recover.

■ **Watering** Never allow the compost in a container to dry out completely.

PLANTING A
LARGE SHRUB

Always take the utmost care not to damage any of the young shoots and leaves

ROOT PRUNING AND REPOTTING A POT-BOUND SHRUB

Withering foliage and poor blooms are often the first signs that your plant has outgrown its container. If you gently ease the plant out of its pot, you are likely to find that the roots have become tightly bound around the soil, forming a stranglehold on the plant. Put it in a slightly larger container and add some fresh soil mix to stimulate growth.

2

1 Gently and carefully remove the shrub from its container. If the pot is jammed full with roots, slide a long-bladed knife between the soil mix and container to free the rootball.

2 Remove the top 2–3-in (5–7.5-cm) layer of soil mix from the surface. Gently tease the soil mix away from the roots, using a handfork if need be, and shake off the old soil.

3 Do not cut the thin fibrous roots, because these are the plant's feeder roots. Prune back about one-quarter of the thicker, nonfibrous roots by up to two-thirds of their length.

4 Gently place the rootball in its pot, and fill in around it with fresh compost. Firm the soil mix down around the roots so that there are no air pockets. Water the shrub well.

WALL-TRAINED SHRUBS

Growing shrubs against a wall or other support not only shows them off to their best advantage but can, in many instances, improve their productivity in terms of flowers or fruit. It is also an invaluable device for livening up a bare expanse of brickwork.

FORMING A FRAMEWORK

2

Training a plant's stem horizontally against a wall concentrates its energies on producing sideshoots along its length, which grow upward with vigor and bear more flowers and fruit. Suitable shrubs include *Cotoneaster horizontalis*, forsythia, summer-flowering jasmine *(Jasminum officinale)*, *Magnolia grandiflora*, pyracantha, solanum, spirea, tamarisk, and wisteria.

Single-stemmed plants, such as ceanothus and chaenomeles, need to be cut back hard when first planted, to encourage branching. Then choose four or five strong stems to form a well-spaced framework of branches against the wall. Cut back any inward- and outward-growing shoots to one or two buds to encourage branches to grow out sideways.

Once established, shorten any stems that have reached the limit of their space, reducing inward- and outward-growing shoots to two to three buds and deadheading on a regular basis.

ADDING INTEREST TO THE HOUSE
The plain walls of a house or cottage can be beautifully enhanced by the addition of a wall-trained shrub such as this colorful wisteria.

Prune established wall shrubs like spirea and tamarisk in early spring by cutting the previous year's shoots back to old wood. This is also the time to thin out old and weak wood on summer-flowering jasmine and solanum. Thin *Magnolia grandiflora* after flowering. Pyracanthas need special attention as their flowers and berries are borne on fruiting sideshoots, called spurs, on old wood. Spring pruning consists of removing any weak, damaged, or unhealthy growth and shortening vigorous new shoots back to two or three leaves. Then, in late summer, remove any new shoots that shield the ripening berries.

PRUNING A WALL-TRAINED CEANOTHUS

1 When the shrub, in this case *Ceanothus* 'Delight', is first planted, prune it back hard to stimulate the growth of strong new shoots. Select four or five of these and train them up and along the wall. Then cut any inward- and outward-facing shoots back to one or two buds.

2 Once the shrub is established against the wall, and flowering freely, remember to deadhead it regularly in order to encourage further flowering. Also keep an eye out for any further inward- and outward-facing shoots, and prune these back as described above.

3 You will also need to prune back any vigorous shoots that are outgrowing the space allotted to the plant. This may involve the removal of strong, healthy growth, but it is necessary to keep the shrub in check and looking its best, and to avoid overcrowding.

PRUNING HEDGES

Formal or informal, deciduous or evergreen, flowering or not, tall or dwarf: the possibilities are seemingly endless when it comes to choosing plants for a hedge. An important factor to consider before you decide is the amount of time and effort they will demand.

LOOKING AT THE OPTIONS

2

Just how much attention a hedge needs depends on the type of plant grown. Small-leaved plants can be trimmed with garden shears or an electric hedge trimmer (always wear protective goggles), but tackle the large-leaved ones with pruning shears to avoid torn leaves. Encourage new hedges to fill out by lightly trimming three or four times a year.

Fast-growing plants like hawthorn *(Crataegus)*, privet *(Ligustrum)*, and *Lonicera nitida* will need regular trimming throughout the milder months of the year to keep them tidy and in check. If you plant the fast-growing Leyland cypress

(× *Cupressocyparis leylandii*), keep it firmly under control. The western red cedar *(Thuja plicata)* has similar foliage but grows much more slowly.

Plants like box *(Buxus)*, hornbeam *(Carpinus)*, escallonia, beech *(Fagus)*, Lawson cypress *(Chamaecyparis lawsoniana)*, *Cotoneaster simonsii*, holly *(Ilex)*, and yew *(Taxus)* need trimming once in summer and again in early fall. If you only have time to trim your hedge once a year, plant *Aucuba japonica*, *Berberis darwinii*, or laurel *(Prunus laurocerasus)*.

FORMAL HEDGE
This hedge of × *Cupressocyparis leylandii* 'Castlewellan' will need a regular trim to keep it neat.

FORMAL HEDGES

You will need to trim a formal hedge with almost military precision on a regular basis if it is to look its best. Remember the rule: the harder the trimming, the denser the hedge.

The top of a formal hedge should be slightly narrower than the base to prevent snow and wind damage. Snow will slide off rather than sink through the middle of the hedge and distort its shape. Sloping sides will also allow more light to reach the bottom of the hedge, encouraging denser growth there. When trimming, therefore, slope the sides of the hedge inward slightly, so that the base is wider than the top. A string guide-line, attached to canes or stakes at both ends of the hedge, will help you produce an even slope.

INFORMAL AND FLOWERING HEDGES

These can take on a much looser shape than the neat, regimented style of a formal hedge, but they do need to be pruned (rather than given an allover trim) to remove any old and dead wood, and to keep them within bounds. The timing of pruning is also more crucial, as you do not want to cut out any developing flower buds. Prune those flowering on the current season's wood in late winter or very early spring, and those flowering on wood formed the previous year immediately after flowering.

Escallonia rubra var. *macrantha* makes a good summer-flowering evergreen hedge, while the evergreen *Viburnum tinus* flowers in late winter. Trim both after flowering.

Deciduous, nonflowering hedges, including beech or hornbeam, should be pruned at the end of the summer to encourage them to retain their leaves during winter. Hedges grown for their decorative display of berries should be pruned in winter, in the case of cotoneaster, or late spring or early summer for pyracantha.

2

FLOWERING HEDGE
The evergreen *Pyracantha rogersiana* bears a profusion of small white flowers in spring, which are followed by orange-red berries later in the year.

2

INFORMAL HEDGE
Deciduous *Philadelphus*
'Manteau d'Hermine'
has a good display of
white flowers and can
be used for a loose-
growing hedge.

PRUNING AND TRIMMING HEDGING PLANTS

HEDGING PLANT	WHEN TO PRUNE	HOW TO PRUNE
Aucuba japonica	Late spring	Remove old stems
Berberis darwinii *Berberis* × *stenophylla*	Early summer after flowering	Trim to shape
Buxus sempervirens (boxwood)	Two or three times in growing season	Trim to shape
Carpinus betulus (hornbeam)	Summer and fall	Trim to encourage leaf retention in winter
Chamaecyparis lawson-iana (Lawson cypress)	Spring and fall	Remove new growth Trim to shape
Cotoneaster simonsii	Winter	Trim if necessary
Crataegus monogyna	Spring, summer, fall	Trim to shape
× *Cupressocyparis leylandii* (Leyland cypress)	Early fall	Trim to shape
Escallonia rubra var. *macrantha*	Late summer, after flowering	Trim to shape
Fagus sylvatica (beech)	Summer and fall	Trim to shape and for winter leaf retention

FORMATIVE PRUNING

In the early years, hedges need attention if they are to stay looking good. The sloping sides of a formal hedge should be formed. The sides of hedges of evergreens or conifers need to be kept tidy, and once the main stems reach the desired height of the hedge, they should be cut back. Most deciduous hedges grow best if cut back by about one-third after planting, and again the next winter. Cut back strong-growing hedges, such as hawthorn or privet, to about 6–12in (15–30cm) in the first spring after planting.

RENOVATING A HEDGE

Where hedges outgrow their space and become straggly or bare at the base, they require drastic pruning, carried out over a couple of years. In early spring, cut plants down hard on one side. Give the other side a standard prune. Trim the top back to about 6in (15cm) below the eventual height of the hedge, then apply feed. The following spring, trim the new shoots and cut the other side of the hedge back hard. The next year should see healthy new growth all over the plant that can be trimmed as usual.

2

PRUNING AND TRIMMING HEDGING PLANTS

HEDGING PLANT	WHEN TO PRUNE	HOW TO PRUNE
Forsythia	Late spring after flowering	Remove old wood, trim to shape
Fuchsia 'Riccartonii'	Spring	Remove old wood, trim to shape
Ilex (holly)	Summer	Trim to shape
Lavandula (lavender)	After flowering	Remove flower heads
Ligustrum (privet)	Two or three times in growing season	Trim to shape
Lonicera nitida (honeysuckle)	Two or three times in growing season	Trim to shape
Prunus laurocerasus (laurel)	Midspring or late summer	Trim to shape
Pyracantha (firethorn)	Midsummer	Remove straggly and overvigorous growth
Taxus baccata (yew)	Midsummer/early fall	Trim to shape
Thuja plicata	Fall	Trim if necessary
Viburnum tinus	Late spring	Cut out old wood

PRUNING TREES

For the most part, trees need little pruning, which is good news because they are perhaps the hardest plants to prune. Large, mature specimens should really be left to a tree surgeon. Always use an approved tree surgeon – one with all the necessary qualifications and insurance coverage. You can tackle any dead or diseased wood on small trees that can be easily reached from the ground, however, and tidy up any straggly growth to improve the overall shape of the tree.

2

WHEN TO PRUNE

It is advisable to prune any large-growing trees while they are still quite young. Prune deciduous trees during the dormant season when they have no leaves – the tree's shape will then be visible, and pruning at that time of the year is less stressful to the tree. Spring is the best season to prune almost all evergreens. Wait until late spring before removing winter-damaged branches, as some regrowth may start as the weather warms up.

The aim when pruning a tree is to create as symmetrical and natural a shape as possible. In order to achieve this, you may need to remove some branches and shorten others.

REMOVING BRANCHES

Trees are often planted in the wrong place, usually where there is not enough space for them as they grow bigger. Where such a tree is causing problems, you may need to remove some branches. Pruning and removing branches may also become necessary as a tree gets older or to improve the shape. Always remove branches cleanly: the cleaner the cut, the lower the risk of disease. Do not take the branch off flush with the trunk. You will notice a little swelling or ridge where the branch meets the trunk, known as the "branch collar" (see below), and any cuts should be made just beyond it. Cut off any larger branches in stages (see opposite).

PRUNING FOR SHAPE

- In fall, first remove any crossing branches the tree may have produced.

- Then take out any dead or weak growth, as well as any branches that are growing in the wrong direction.

- Lightly prune the remaining growth into the desired shape.

- In order to restrict the height of a tree and allow more light into the center, take out the leading branch or trunk at the desired final height.

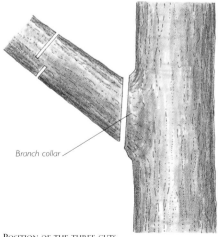

Branch collar

POSITION OF THE THREE CUTS

1 Take the branch back little by little to relieve as much of the weight as possible. About 12in (30cm) from the trunk, saw a quarter of the way into the final section, cutting upward toward the center of the branch. This stops the bark from tearing.

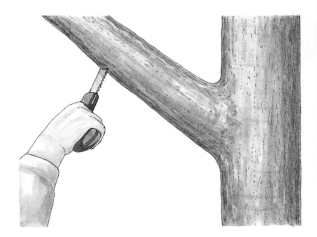

2

2 Make a second cut 2in (5cm) away from the first cut. Point the blade downward, and away from the trunk. Saw until the two cuts meet and the section falls away.

3 The final cut should be made just beyond the branch collar, taking care not to cut into the bark ridge itself. Clean up any rough sawn edges using a pruning knife. Applying a sealant to the cut area is not now thought to be necessary. The wound should be left to callus over and heal itself.

2

UNWANTED GROWTHS

Where trees have been grafted onto another rootstock – such as some flowering cherries *(Prunus)*, crab apples *(Malus)*, lilacs *(Syringa)*, and many weeping forms – suckers may appear at the base. Remove these, and any water shoots, as soon as you see them (see p. 9).

Witches' broom is a deformity that causes some trees to develop clusters of stunted shoots. Birches, cherries, hornbeams, and plums are among trees affected. Although not harmful, these twiggy lumps are unsightly on ornamental trees and may cause poor fruiting. They can be removed in winter, when the tree is dormant, by cutting off the affected branches 6in (15cm) below the growth.

POLLARDED WILLOWS
These willows *(Salix)* have been pollarded to restrict their size and create a dense head of branches and foliage, making a compact tree.

POLLARDING

The technique known as pollarding is used to restrict the size of a tree that has outgrown its position. It is a form of hard pruning that suits only a few types of tree, and is most often carried out on limes *(Tilia)* and willows *(Salix)*. All of the tree's branches are cut back to the trunk every few years (see below left).

ROOT PRUNING

Pruning tree roots encourages new roots to grow, enabling the plant to establish itself much more quickly, and is carried out prior to planting bare-rooted trees, as well as shrubs and roses, or before moving them to another position. It is best to do it during a mild spell in fall or winter. Shorten long, straggly roots to make planting easier, and remove any dead, diseased, damaged, or crossing roots to leave an untangled, even distribution of healthy roots.

Fast-growing trees and shrubs can be root-pruned *in situ* (this is also a remedial measure you can take when fruit trees produce too much strong topgrowth at the expense of fruiting). The thin, fibrous roots, by which the plant feeds, should be disturbed as little as possible. It is the thicker anchoring roots that need attention. If the tree is large, carry out the job in two stages: half one winter, and half the following year.

Dig a trench 3ft (1m) or so away from the trunk of the tree, about 18in (45cm) deep and 12in (30cm) wide. Remove the soil from the trench carefully to expose the roots. Cut through the large, woody anchoring roots with a pruning saw. Then replace the soil and firm it well. Stake an immature tree to prevent wind-rock. In spring, feed and water the tree during any dry spells.

2

PLEACHING

A traditional way of training young trees, such as beeches *(Fagus)*, hornbeams *(Carpinus betulus)*, or limes *(Tilia)*, is pleaching. The trees are grown against a framework of supporting posts and wires, to form a screen or canopy of interwoven branches with a clear row of separate individual trunks beneath. It is a slow and very high-maintenance operation that involves pruning, supporting, and intertwining the branches in fall, and clipping the foliage in summer to maintain the shape, over a period of several years.

Once established, the framework can be removed and the trees just need regular clipping as for an ordinary hedge. Some flowering shrubs, such as laburnum and wisteria, can be pleached to form a flowering arch or tunnel.

CREATING FORMALITY
Limes *(Tilia)* are good for pleaching, especially in a formal setting. The bare, regimented trunks provide strong vertical emphasis.

TREE PRESERVATION

Before carrying out any major tree surgery, check that the tree is not subject to any local or state conservation laws. If it is, you need permission before cutting off a single branch. Permission will not usually be withheld if the tree or any of its limbs are a danger to life or property. By the same token, if the necessary work may affect overhead wires or under-ground cables, the relevant utility provider must be informed. In this instance, the work should be done by a qualified tree surgeon.

CONIFERS

Mature conifers need little or no pruning, but there are some routine tasks you can undertake in order to keep them looking their best.

■ **Splayed growth** Conifers are often prized for their strong shape and clean lines, so it is particularly annoying when branches are pushed out of line by settled snow, wind, or just the weight of an upright branch. To regain the shape of your tree, tie the splayed branch back into the main stem using soft garden twine.

■ **Dead patches** Small brown patches of dead foliage can be trimmed off using pruning shears, but any larger ones may require a little more ingenuity, especially if they disrupt the profile of a shaped conifer. New growth on conifers does not shoot from old wood. After completely removing the dead growth, cover the hole left by bending neighboring branches over the gap and tying them to a cane or stake secured to the main stem or branch. New growth on these branches should soon hide the cane and cover the hole.

1 From time to time, patches of brown foliage may appear on your conifer. This is likely to be damaged or scorched growth and should be removed. If the patch is small, cut out all of the dead foliage with pruning shears.

2 If the area of dead growth is likely to leave a large hole or disrupt the tree's profile, make amends by bending over nearby shoots or branches to cover the hole, and tie them in place with soft twine.

Warning

If you want to remove overhanging growth from a tree or large shrub that belongs to a neighboring property, you are entitled to do so. However, you may remove only as much of a branch as is growing over a line drawn upward from your boundary. It would be both wise and courteous to inform your neighbor of your intentions before you start cutting the overhanging growth, at which time the disposal of any prunings can be agreed upon.

ROSES

Pruning roses is not the mysterious art form that many people think it is, but the various different types do have their own specific needs. This chapter provides a simple set of guidelines for each type in order for you to be confident of carrying out pruning correctly.

Having dealt with the annual pruning routine, there are also one or two regular maintenance operations that need to be tackled, such as removing suckers and deadheading. A quick rundown of necessary seasonal tasks concludes the chapter.

Remember that for rose pruning you will need some sharp pruning shears and, very importantly, a pair of heavy-duty garden gloves – most roses have thorns and you will find that they will be much easier to prune if you are not constantly worried about being pricked.

3

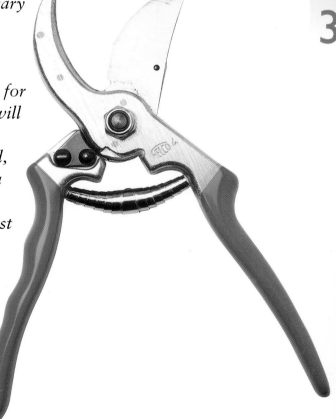

PRUNING ROSES

Roses are in a class of their own when it comes to pruning as the various types have their own different needs. If you want them to perform at their very best, giving a stunning show of color and sometimes also fragrance, it is best to give them a helping hand.

WHEN TO PRUNE

Late winter or early spring is the best time to prune repeat-flowering roses, when the plants are dormant or new growth is just beginning to show. Prune too early and new growth will risk being tipped by frost, and you will then have to prune again, cutting back to undamaged wood.

Ramblers should be pruned once flowering has finished, that is in late summer or early fall. Established roses can be pruned at the beginning of winter, too, but bear in mind

MODERN SHRUB ROSE
'Octavia Hill' is an example of a Modern shrub rose (see p. 51). It produces a profusion of fragrant pink blooms from summer to fall.

that, although this may be fine in a sheltered, warm garden, in colder, more exposed spots heavy pruning at this time may lessen a plant's chances of survival. The best advice, therefore, for all areas, is to give roses a light pruning at the end of their season.

Shorten the stems of large- and cluster-flowered, tall-shrub, and climbing types by about one-third, and finish the job when the weather improves during the spring. The light, prewinter pruning will help to protect the plant from the damaging effects of winter winds, particularly in exposed sites or coastal gardens.

PRUNING A NEWLY PLANTED ROSE BUSH

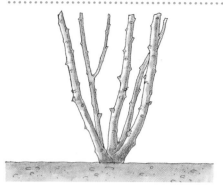
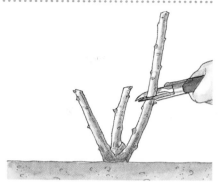

1 Once a rose has been planted, you will need to prune it back quite hard to stimulate healthy growth from low down. These stems are long and some are crossing and even damaged.

2 Prune each shoot down to about 3–6in (7–15cm) above the base. Make a slanting cut just above an outward-facing bud, so that the new growth forms an open-centered bush.

3

HOW TO PRUNE ESTABLISHED ROSES

All roses need pruning to develop their shape, to control their size and vigor, to help them remain healthy, and to encourage flowering. Remove old and spindly growth regularly, cutting as low down on the plant as possible, to make room for new growth to sprout from the base. Reducing strong, healthy growths by about one-third will encourage side growth. It will also lessen the risk of damage from wind-rock, which can cause broken shoots and weakened stems.

The aim is to create an open-centered plant, giving space, light, and air to the stems so that they can develop freely. Always use a pair of sharp pruning shears and wear gloves. Cut back to a dormant, outward-facing bud to encourage an upward and outward growth habit. Make each cut at an angle, sloping down and away from the bud, leaving a clean edge. After pruning, apply a layer of rose fertilizer, watering it in if the ground is dry, followed by a mulch to prevent moisture loss.

■ **Dead and diseased growth** Cut right back to healthy wood – the cut surface will be white rather than brown.

■ **Weak growth and spindly stems** You should remove all of these so that the plant can concentrate its energy on the good shoots.

■ **Crossing and inward-growing stems** Removing these will prevent overcrowding, which would otherwise hinder healthy growth.

FALL INTEREST

Roses that produce ornamental hips in late summer or fall, such as *Rosa rugosa* 'Alba' and *R.* 'Frau Dagmar Hastrup,' should not be pruned until late winter or early spring.

ROSE CATEGORIES

For pruning purposes, roses can be divided into seven quite distinct categories. These are: modern bush roses, including both the large-flowered (hybrid tea) and cluster-flowered (floribunda) types; climbing and rambling roses; old garden roses; modern shrub roses; standard roses; ground-cover roses; and miniature bush roses.

MODERN BUSH ROSES

This general category includes the large-flowered (or hybrid tea) and cluster-flowered (or floribunda) roses. The aim when pruning these bush roses is to encourage plenty of new shoots that will bear a long succession of blooms throughout the summer. They need pruning annually.

3

■ **Newly planted bush roses** Prune these back hard to within 4–6in (10–15cm) of the ground, to leave three or four buds on each stem. Do this as soon as the bushes are planted in fall. This will allow a strong root system to develop and will also encourage strong new branches to form near the base of the plant.

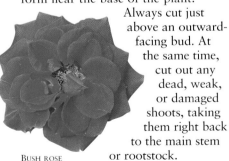

Always cut just above an outward-facing bud. At the same time, cut out any dead, weak, or damaged shoots, taking them right back to the main stem or rootstock.

BUSH ROSE

■ **Established roses** Prune established roses each spring, while the plants are still dormant. First, cut back all frost-damaged, diseased, and old stems to healthy wood. Dead wood is brown and dry inside, even though it may still be green outside. Remove any twiggy and crowded growth.

■ **Container-grown roses** If these are planted in the growing season, do not prune them quite so severely; remove any open flowers and damaged growth.

■ **Large-flowered (hybrid tea) roses** Reduce the remaining healthy stems of these roses by about one-half to two-thirds of their length, leaving them about 8–10in (20–25cm) from the ground. More vigorous varieties need a lighter pruning, otherwise they will bear plenty of leaves but few flowers.

■ **Cluster-flowered (floribunda) roses** Prune lightly, cutting shoots back by no more than one-third to one-half of their length, or to about 10–12in (25–30cm) from the ground. Cut some older wood almost down to ground level for better flowering next year. The harder you prune these roses, the larger the blooms, albeit fewer of them. For quantity rather than size, prune lightly. Always angle cuts to 45°, about ¼in (6mm) above an outward-pointing bud.

TIP
Remember to protect your hands with a pair of sturdy gardening gloves, preferably those with reinforced finger pads, to avoid injury from rose thorns.

TRIMMING BUSH ROSES

1 Tall stems are prone to wind damage in late fall. Wind-rock also loosens the roots, leaving a gap where water may collect and freeze.

2 Cut the stems back so that their height is halved and firm the soil around the roots. This strengthens the plant's resistance to wind-rock.

3

CLIMBING AND RAMBLING ROSES

The aim when pruning climbing and rambling roses is to achieve a balance between growth and flowers. These roses need careful pruning in early spring to restrict their height and spread and to keep the flowers coming evenly across the plant, not just at the very top.

Although ramblers and climbers may seem similar, there are some differences, and these affect their pruning needs; the ramblers require slightly more attention than the climbers. A true rambler can be distinguished from climbing roses by the many new shoots that sprout from the base while the plant is in full bloom. Do not cut these away as they are the stems that will bloom the following year.

Plants of both types need little pruning, but some careful training is necessary in the early stages. When first planted, just remove any dead or damaged stems and spindly growth. In the case of ramblers, cut stems down to 15in (45cm) if this has not already been done. As the stems grow, tie them into the support; the more horizontal the stem the more flowers it will produce. In subsequent years, continue to train new growth while it is still young and pliable.

■ **Ramblers** Roses such as 'Félicité Perpétue' and 'Albertine' carry their huge trusses of small flowers on long, flexible stems formed from the base each year. Although they produce a more colourful mass of blooms than climbers, they usually only flower once, and may only last for a couple of weeks or so. Because ramblers flower mainly on the previous year's growth, they should be cut back after flowering, in late summer.

3

'CLIMBING ICEBERG'
The white flowers of
this climbing rose look
spectacular when trained
to grow up and over a
red-brick wall.

Cut down to ground level one-third of the older flowering stems. Tie in the new growth to a support and train it horizontally. Cut back sideshoots above a healthy shoot to within two to four buds of the main stem. Curb any excess growth by shortening shoots.

■ **Climbers**   Roses such as 'Golden Showers' and 'Zéphirine Drouhin' have stiffer stems and smaller flower clusters than ramblers but the individual flowers are larger and there may be two or more flushes of bloom from early summer until the first frosts. Flowers are borne mainly on sideshoots, on a permanent framework of mature wood that needs to be tied to a support. Annual pruning stimulates better flowering.

After climbers have flowered for the first time, trim sideshoots by a half in the fall. This will provide a strong framework with which to cover the support. Any main shoots that have outgrown their space can be tidied up at this time.

In the early years, cut back all sideshoots by about two-thirds, or to two or three strong buds, in early spring. Prune back shorter sideshoots that have flowered the previous summer by half or to within a bud or two of the main stem.

Once climbers have established themselves, they need only light pruning to keep them in check. The removal of dead or diseased wood along with regular deadheading will suffice. Overlong shoots can be shortened at any time.

RENOVATING AN OLD CLIMBER

If your garden contains a neglected climbing rose, try renovating it in early fall. First cut out any diseased and leggy bare stems, if necessary down to ground level or at least back to a strong stem. Then cut back one or two older, unproductive stems to a healthy shoot or bud, within 12in (30cm) or so of the ground. You may need to use loppers on thicker wood. This will encourage fresh new shoots to form at ground level, as well as flowering lower down on the plant. Reduce the remaining strong new stems by at least half of their length.

OLD GARDEN ROSES

The majority of old garden roses should be treated like shrubs and pruned only lightly to keep them in shape after their single flush of flowers is over. Those that flower more than once in a season should be pruned when dormant in early spring. The method of pruning is the same in both instances.

■ **Newly planted** These need no pruning except to remove any dead, damaged, or badly placed shoots, while any overlong stems can be shortened by about one-third of their length. In spring, cut out any wood that has succumbed to frost, cutting back to a good bud on sound, green wood, and remove all weak and diseased stems and any that are crossing or badly placed.

■ **Naturally rounded habit** After flowering, simply shorten the lateral stems (side growths) back to a sideshoot or bud, 3–6in (7.5–15cm) from the main stem. If the bush becomes congested, take out two or three of the oldest main stems from the base.

'FERDINAND PICHARD'
This is a fine example of an old garden shrub rose, with plenty of fragrant, pink flowers that have distinctive darker stripes on the petals.

■ **More spreading habit** Old main stems and laterals can be shortened by about one-third of their length, cutting back to a healthy bud or sideshoot. Also remove any shoots that arch over and touch the ground. In fall, it is a good idea to shorten any long leggy shoots by up to one-third to prevent them being damaged by winter winds (see Trimming bush roses, p. 49).

MODERN SHRUB ROSES

Repeat-flowering types of modern shrub rose, such as 'Ballerina' and 'Graham Thomas,' require only the minimum of attention. The leading shoots of established bushes benefit by being cut back by up to one-third of their length during their dormant period in early spring, while some stems may need thinning if they have become overcrowded. In time, older stems should be removed to encourage the production of new growth.

3

3

STANDARD ROSES

Standards are pruned according to the type of rose used: large-flowered, cluster-flowered, or miniature. The aim is to create a balanced head and, as with all other roses, to cut out all dead, diseased, and damaged wood along with any crossing shoots.

■ **Newly planted standard roses** These should be cut back to within 8–10in (20–25cm) of the main stem (graft union), cutting just above a healthy bud.

■ **Established standards** Remove all dead and crossing wood and take out some of the older wood in order to maintain a balanced, compact head. This will also encourage the rose to produce vigorous new flowering shoots. Cut back main branches by half their length, and sideshoots back to two or three buds.

■ **Once-flowering types** Prune after flowering has finished.

■ **Repeat-flowering types** Prune in early spring, while still dormant. It is also a good idea, in exposed spots, to trim back growth in fall, to reduce the risk of damage from strong winter winds.

■ **Weeping standards** These need no pruning to begin with, other than to remove dead, diseased, and damaged wood and to take back any weak shoots to a strong bud. Then, after a couple of years, each fall remove the oldest flowering branches to encourage the growth of new wood. In spring, lightly cut back the new growth, which will encourage the formation of sideshoots. Any growing tips of shoots that touch the ground should be lightly cut back.

GROUND-COVER ROSES

Ground-cover roses, such as the 'Flower Carpet' kinds, do not really require any pruning, but you can clip them over lightly with hand shears in spring. Repeat-flowering types should be tidied up in early spring, but wait until after flowering for the rest. Then cut out any dead, diseased, or crossing stems, and shorten any stems that outgrow their space.

'RED BLANKET'
Ground-cover roses have a low, spreading habit, and they need little pruning other than light trimming to give of their best.

STANDARD STEM
Keep the stem of a standard clear by rubbing or pulling off any shoots that appear during the season.

3

Miniature roses

In spite of their size, miniature roses such as 'Baby Masquerade' and 'Starina' do need pruning. Think of them as smaller versions of the large- or cluster-flowered roses and apply the same principles of pruning: prune hard when first planted, down to 2–3in (5–7.5cm) above the ground, and then annually. You should also remember to deadhead spent blooms on a regular basis.

During their dormant period, cut main stems back to four or five buds from the base, or about half to two-thirds of their length, and prune sideshoots back to within one or two buds of the main stem. In addition,

'TEAR DROP'
Miniature roses are ideal for growing in containers on a patio or terrace, especially in smaller gardens.

completely remove any weak, crossing, diseased, or dead stems. Watch out for any water shoots, or vigorous growths out of scale with the rest of the plant, and remove them as soon as they are seen.

PRUNING MINIATURES

You may find it easier to use scissors, rather than pruning shears, when you are pruning miniature roses.

ROUTINE ROSE CARE

As well as the annual pruning routine, roses also need some seasonal maintenance to keep them blooming and healthy. Deadheading spent blooms ensures you a second flush of flowers or an extended flowering season, while removing suckers means that the plant's energy is focused on producing new growth and blooms rather than being drained by rogue shoots.

REMOVING SUCKERS

Keep an eye out for suckers on budded or grafted roses, which grow from the ground or from below the graft on the stem. Look for shoots that differ from the rest in color, size, feel, or foliage. Suckers should be removed as soon as they emerge by pulling rather than cutting.

> **Warning**
>
> If you do have to remove a rose, do not plant another rose in the same place because of the risk of replant disease, which causes stunted growth.

3

1 When you find a sucker growing out from the base of a rose (here it can be seen in the foreground, with paler green leaves), remove the soil around it with a trowel until you can see where it originates on the plant.

2 Wearing a pair of heavy-duty gloves to protect your hands from thorns, grab hold of the sucker as close to its point of origin as possible, and pull it away sharply. It should come off cleanly.

DEADHEADING

A form of pruning, deadheading involves removing spent blooms with either pruning shears or scissors. This will prolong the flowering of your roses, encouraging a second flush. When you cut off each dead bloom, the next bud in the bunch is encouraged to open, while at the same time growth in buds lower down the stem is stimulated.

Once all the flower buds in a cluster are past their best, remove some of the stem as well, cutting it back to the second or third bud down the stem to just above a swelling bud from which a new shoot will grow. Do not cut back too far; no more than 12in (30cm) should suffice. At the same time, you might want to cut back any stems that are spoiling the shape of the bush.

OLD ROSE BUSHES

Neglected, ageing bushes, with spindly stems that are devoid of leaf except at the very top, may be given a fresh lease on life by employing the following "kill-or-cure" technique.

■ During the dormant season (late fall to early spring), remove all dead, diseased, and weak stems right down to the base of the plant.

■ Take older main stems back to strong new shoots close to the base.

■ Shorten remaining strong stems by at least half their length. Vary the

3

DEADHEADING
To encourage the production of a large number of flowers, over a long period, remove any dead or fading flowers as soon as you can.

height of stems to encourage new growth at different levels.

■ Saw off any dead stumps flush with the ground; otherwise rainwater may collect in the stump and encourage rot to set in.

■ In spring, apply a general fertilizer around the root area. Water this in and then apply a mulch.

■ Continue to feed, weed, and water throughout spring and summer.

■ If the plant recovers into a healthy specimen with strong new shoots, you can then prune as normal.

HIPS AND SEEDHEADS

Remember not to deadhead any of those roses that produce either hips or decorative fall seed heads.

3

SEASONAL CHECKLIST

TIME	TASK
Early spring	As the weather warms up, start to prune both cluster- and large-flowered rose bushes as well as true climbing roses.
	Check all other roses for frost damage and prune out any that is visible.
Early summer	Check for suckers around the base of roses. They should be pulled away from the plant rather than cut off (see p. 54).
Midsummer	Thin out the oldest stems from single-flowering rambling and shrub roses once blooms fade.
	Lightly prune large-flowered roses to keep them tidy and flowering.
Summer/fall	Keep on top of the task of deadheading on repeat-flowering types of roses to encourage a further flush of blooms.
	Leave flower heads on those roses with fall hips, such as *Rosa glauca* and *R. rugosa*.
Late summer/early fall	Prune rambling roses.
Midfall	Tie in loose shoots and branches of climbing roses and remove any straggly or long stems.
	Lightly prune other roses, finishing the job in early spring.
Late fall through winter	Pot-ready and bare-rooted roses should be planted in mild weather and when the ground is not frozen. Bush roses should be pruned hard, and any dead or damaged wood removed.

BUSH ROSES

CLIMBING PLANTS

Pruning and training come into their own when you are dealing with this special group of garden plants. If left alone, climbers will continue their quest ever upward toward the light, producing masses of leafy growth at the expense of flowers and fruit. In order to produce the best show possible they need a little help. In this chapter, the why, when, and how of pruning climbers is dealt with first, before the question of the right support for each group is looked at.

When it comes to pruning, clematis seems to cause more problems than almost any other climbing plant, so the specific needs of the three main groups are clearly explained. Honeysuckle and wisteria are examined in more detail too, as are the more rampant climbers such as Virginia creeper. The chapter ends by taking a look at climbers that have been trained against a wall, and how best to keep them both within bounds and performing well.

4

PRUNING CLIMBERS

Careful pruning and training, especially early on, are essential for success with climbing plants. Most mature climbers can be left unpruned until they outgrow their welcome; an annual tidy-up to cut them down to size should suffice.

WHEN TO PRUNE

All newly planted climbers need some pruning and tying in for their first few years to encourage them to produce a sturdy, vigorous, and well-shaped framework of stems. Mature climbers will require varying degrees of routine pruning (see p. 60) if they are to continue to grow and flower well. If they are pruned regularly, and not left to become congested, climbing plants will be much healthier and bloom more freely.

The flowering season and the age of the wood on which the flowers are produced dictate when a climber should be pruned. In all cases, after pruning, tie in the remaining shoots to establish a balanced framework of stems. Take great care, however, not to tie the shoot so tightly that it cuts into the "flesh" (see p. 60), creating an open wound.

■ **Evergreen or fast-growing climbers** Prune these plants in summer in order to restrict their growth.

■ **Old wood** Prune those climbers that flower on the previous year's (or even older) growth, as soon as flowering is over. Take out any weak or damaged growth and remove any stems that are crossing or congested. Cut these flush with the main trunk or stem or just above a healthy bud. Flowered wood should be pruned back to a vigorous shoot or bud, which will encourage new shoots to develop and ripen before the winter.

■ **New wood** Climbers that flower on new wood are best pruned at the end of winter or in early spring when the plant is still in its dormant period, but do not take up your pruning shears during any snaps of cold, frosty weather.

■ **Alternate buds** For climbers with alternate bud arrangements (see p. 16), make a sloping cut just above a healthy, plump bud that is pointing toward the direction in which you want the new shoot to grow.

■ **Opposite buds** For climbers with opposite-facing buds (see p. 16), make a straight cut above a pair of healthy buds, taking great care not to damage the buds.

■ **Dead and damaged wood** Remove all dead, damaged, and congested wood to open out the plant and reduce the risk of disease. Prune back the sideshoots to four or six buds. This will encourage strong new growth and flower spurs, as well as keeping the plant in check.

FRUITING PLANTS

Some climbers, such as *Billardiera longiflora*, are grown mainly for their attractive fruits. Lightly prune after flowering to remove any damaged growth, leaving some fruiting stems.

FORMATIVE PRUNING

When pruning and training climbers, you should aim to stimulate the production of healthy new growth, to create a balance between new growth and quality flowering, and to keep the plant within its allotted growing space. All of this may mean removing larger stems, spacing stems more evenly, or tying in stems to the chosen support in order to encourage a better-shaped plant.

Before planting any climber, cut out dead, damaged, and weak growth. If the climber will only need one main stem, leave the strongest one, and cut away the rest. Wait a season before checking the growth of this single stem, and then cut it down almost to ground level in the following early spring. Such hard pruning promotes new growth at the base of the plant. To encourage more than one strong stem on a climber, pinch out the growing tips of existing stems. This will stimulate branching at the base of the plant.

Little or no pruning should be necessary in the first few years of a climber's life.

ROSES AND CLEMATIS
If you have the space, the combination of a climbing rose and a clematis with flowers in a contrasting color can be stunning.

4

Shoots need to be trained and tied in, in order to develop a well-spaced framework. The growing tips of vigorous leading shoots can be cut back to encourage them to branch. Where growth is sparse, particularly at the base of a climbing plant, branching can be encouraged by shortening shoots to leave three to six buds in that area. Also cut out wayward shoots and any that are growing in an undesirable direction.

ESTABLISHED CLIMBERS

Most mature climbers can be left unpruned until they become untidy. Even then, they do not need the same kind of precise pruning that is so necessary for roses, for example. In general, an annual tidy-up to cut them back down to size should suffice. These stems will be replaced by younger shoots, growing out either from ground level or from quite low down on the old stem. At the same time, clear away any

---

ROUTINE PRUNING

• Remove dead and diseased wood.

• Cut out old growth to promote new growth or better flowering.

• Deadhead flowering climbers.

• Remember the rule: prune flowering climbers after flowering; and non-flowering types in spring or summer.

---

debris, such as dead leaves and twigs, that has become trapped by, or attached to, the support, because this could be harboring pests and diseases.

If left unchecked and unpruned, most climbers will eventually become a tangled, congested mass of dead

DAMAGE FROM AN OVERTIGHT TIE
This ceanothus has been badly scarred. When tying in shoots, make sure that the tie is loose enough for the growing shoot to expand.

and twiggy growth. A climber in this state is not only unsightly but may be too heavy for its support or causing a nuisance. Careful pruning should remedy the situation, but it will take time. The climber may recover from being cut back right to its base, but it would be better to tackle such drastic pruning over a period of a few years.

■ **First year** Remove as much of the oldest wood as possible, pruning out all the large, woody stems right down to the base of the plant. Take care not to cut any new growth.

Plants like Russian vine *(Fallopia baldschuanica)* can be tackled with garden shears. Taking care to avoid any new growth on top, trim out all the old, dead, and damaged stems from underneath. You may lose some flowering stems for one season, but they will recover to flower the next.

■ **Following years** Cut back one-third of the main stems to ground level. Clear away dead, diseased, and damaged wood, and any debris from the support, as this may harbor pests or diseases. As new growth appears, tie it in to fill any gaps.

WORKING AROUND SUPPORTS

Self-clinging climbers, such as the climbing hydrangea *(Hydrangea petiolaris)*, can be pruned *in situ*, against the wall or fence. For twining or tendril climbers, such as clematis, the task of pruning will be much easier and more thorough if the plants are first detached from their support. Cut through any ties or carefully unwind coiled tendrils.

Main stems or branches that are old and bare should be cut out completely.

As with training young plants, always make sure that you use soft twine and large loops when tying plants back in to avoid causing open wounds. Use a figure-eight tying action to prevent any abrasion between the stem and the support.

4

HORIZONTAL TRAINING

When left to their own devices, climbers will naturally grow upward toward the light. They will need help if they are to send out shoots sideways. This requires you to train some of the shoots to grow horizontally by tying them in along a system of wires, or to a length of trellis which in turn will stimulate flowering and fruiting.

PASSIFLORA

SUPPORTING PLANTS

Careful pruning and strong supports, especially early on, are essential for success with wall-trained, shaped, and climbing plants. Good supports include brick walls, trellises, arches, and screens, but they need to be appropriate for the type of plant.

FRAMES AND SUPPORTS

■ **Arches and arbors** These supports lend themselves to being festooned by clematis, honeysuckle, or roses, but take care that there are no vicious thorns to attack unwary passersby. Any fast-growing plants need some attention to keep them under control. They should be pruned at least once a year, and trained and tied in when young.

■ **Trellises and screens** These supports suit plants that are not natural climbers, such as roses or twinter jasmine *(Jasminum nudiflorum)*, which do not have the means to attach themselves to their support. All new growth needs to be carefully tied in to train the plant up and across the screen or trellis.

■ **Pergolas** Plants such as clematis, wisteria, and the grapevine *(Vitis vinifera)* twine their stems around a support and are ideal for cloaking a freestanding structure such as a pergola. They can also clothe an arbor.

■ **Walls** *Hydrangea petiolaris*, ivies *(Hedera)*, and other self-clinging climbers are best grown against a wall, which will provide a suitable surface for their aerial roots or sucker pads to cling to.

■ **Wire and support** Plants that attach themselves to a support by means of tendrils, for example the passionflower *(Passiflora caerulea)*, need either a system of support wires to coil their tendrils around or a host plant to cling to. Before growing a tendril climber through another plant, however, always take into account how vigorous the climber is likely to be, to ensure that there is no chance of it overpowering its host.

■ **Screens** To hide an eyesore or to grow over an unsightly structure, choose fast-growers such as Russian vine *(Fallopia baldschuanica)* or Virginia creeper *(Parthenocissus quinquefolia)* and Boston ivy *(P. tricuspidata)*. Remember that the rapid growth will need constant cutting back in order to keep the plants within bounds, otherwise it will swamp nearby vegetation.

4

STURDY SUPPORT

Always make sure that the structure or support is sturdy and large enough to accommodate the mature plant. For example, the fast-growing laburnum is ideal for training as a golden arch or tunnel but it must have a strong, preferably metal, framework that is able to take the weight of fully grown trees.

LABURNUM ARCH
When in bloom, trained laburnum creates an extended arch of dazzling golden flowers, through which to stroll during early summer.

4

POPULAR CLIMBERS

There are a few climbing plants that need slightly more attention than most of the others, and these just happen to be some of the most popular climbers we grow in our gardens, including clematis, honeysuckle, wisteria, Russian vine, and Virginia creeper.

CLEMATIS

Pruning clematis is a task that fills many inexperienced gardeners with alarm. The actual pruning process is straightforward enough, but you will need to identify which type of clematis you have because the different types have different pruning requirements. If you do get it wrong, however, the worst that can happen is that you get few, if any, flowers in the following year, and you can then prune correctly.

When grown on walls or supported on a trellis, clematis needs hard pruning each year. This will induce it to produce flowers all over the plant, from the base upward. When it is grown into other plants, it can, generally speaking, be left to its own devices. In this instance, left unpruned, it will flower at the ends

of its branches, where it will be seen against the host plant. For pruning purposes, clematis plants can be divided into three groups.

■ **Early flowering, small-flowered**
This type produces flowers in spring or early summer on the previous year's growth, and you should prune immediately after flowering. *Clematis alpina* and *C. macropetala* need just enough pruning to keep them in check. Remove dead and damaged stems of *C. armandii* and *C. cirrhosa*, and thin out any overcrowded ones, cutting back to the point of origin.

CLEMATIS 'CORRY'
This is an example of a late-flowering clematis, with small flowers borne on the current season's growth. It needs pruning in spring.

The exception in this group is the popular late spring-flowering *C. montana*, which is very vigorous. Where space allows, it requires very little pruning, but in more confined spaces you should cut back the main stem after flowering to within 12in (30cm) of the ground.

CLEMATIS
'NELLY MOSER'

■ **Early flowering, large-flowered** Clematis such as 'Nelly Moser' and 'The President' flower mainly on wood produced the previous year, and should be lightly pruned before new growth appears in early spring. Remove dead, diseased, and straggly growth, then cut back one-third of the remaining stems to a strong pair of buds about 12in (30cm) from the ground. Remember that the largest flowers will be produced on old wood, so do not remove too much.

To restrict the spread of the plant, and to encourage more flowering sideshoots, you can also shorten the remaining long stems back to a strong pair of buds.

■ **Summer- or late-flowering** This type produces its blooms (some have large flowers, some small) on the current season's growth.

'Jackmanii', *C. tangutica*, and *C. viticella* should be cut back hard, to just above the two lowest pairs of healthy leaf buds on each stem. You will need to steel yourself because this will mean cutting the plant down to about 12in (30cm) from the ground. Do this in the early spring before new growth appears. As the new growth develops, tie it to the support at regular intervals. Take care, since these new stems will be fragile and liable to snap off.

To maintain a larger plant, and to stimulate more flowers, leave the main framework of stems alone and prune back just the sideshoots to one pair of buds from the stem. After pruning, apply mulch around the base of the plant, and tie new shoots to the support as they appear.

4

CLEMATIS VARIETIES BY CATEGORY

Early flowering, small-flowered	Summer- or late-flowering
C. alpina	'Alba Luxurians'
C. armandii	'Bill MacKenzie'
C. cirrhosa	'Ernest Markham'
C. macropetala	'Etoile Violette'
C. montana	'Hagley Hybrid'
	'Jackmanii'
Early flowering, large-flowered	'Lady Betty Balfour'
'Beauty of Worcester'	'Perle d'Azur'
'Henryi'	'Star of India'
'Lasurstern'	C. tangutica
'Richard Pennell'	'Ville de Lyon'
'Rouge Cardinal'	C. viticella

HONEYSUCKLE

There are many kinds of honeysuckle *(Lonicera)*, ranging from deciduous, semi-evergreen, or evergreen shrubs, such as fly honeysuckle *(L. xylosteum)*, *L. nitida*, and *L. tatarica*, to woody-stemmed twining climbers. These include Japanese honeysuckle *(L. japonica)* and common honeysuckle or woodbine *(L. periclymenum)*.

Grown mainly for their flowers, which are often fragrant, honeysuckles are a deservedly popular choice of climber for growing up house walls and over pergolas and arches, where their fragrance can be best appreciated. Some species produce glossy berries after flowering, which prolong the plant's ornamental value.

Honeysuckles tend to grow rather rapidly, however, and need pruning annually. To do this, cut out flowered wood, after flowering has finished, in late summer or early fall.

■ **Pruning neglected honeysuckles**
If left alone, climbing honeysuckles will soon become a tangled mess of dead stems and twigs. Any foliage and flowers are borne very high where they cannot be best appreciated. When a honeysuckle reaches this stage, drastic action is called for. Cut one or two of the main stems right back to ground level. If necessary, unravel the growth from its support. Remove dead and diseased wood, making sure to cut cleanly. When pruning is complete, tie the growth back onto its support.

You may find that this is too difficult or time consuming. Instead, try clipping back any unwanted growth using a pair of hand shears. This will keep the plant in shape.

HEALTHY HONEYSUCKLE
This honeysuckle is growing very strongly and producing lots of flowers. It will need regular attention, however, to keep it in check.

Warning

If you neglect to prune your wisteria, even for just one season, the result will be masses of leafy green shoots and no flowers. These are high-maintenance plants, perhaps, but the masses of scented mauve or white flowers in early summer will more than repay your efforts.

WISTERIA

It can take seven years or more for a newly established wisteria to flower, but a strict pruning regime will stimulate the production of short, flowering shoots, rather than long, whippy, nonflowering growths.

Wisteria needs pruning twice a year: first in summer, a couple of months after flowering, and again in midwinter. In summer, cut back all the long new shoots to within five or six buds, or 9in (23cm), of the main branch. In winter, when the plant is dormant, cut these shoots back to two buds. This treatment will encourage the production of shorter flowering spurs rather than long shoots that bear only foliage.

RAMPANT GROWERS

■ **Russian vine** Also known as the mile-a-minute vine, this climber *(Fallopia baldschuanica)* is often planted to cover a fence or unsightly structure quickly, and it lives up to its name. To prevent it becoming a tangled mass, cut some vines down to ground level each spring.

■ **Boston ivy** The Boston ivy *(Parthenocissus tricuspidata)* is a vigorous, self-clinging climber that forms a dense covering and can reach 65ft (20m). To curb its rampant

VIRGINIA CREEPER
Fast-growing Virginia creeper *(Parthenocissus quinquefolia)* provides fairly rapid cover for walls, and has excellent fall foliage color.

4

tendencies, roots can be hard pruned during the dormant period, while in summer, if the plant is being grown against a house wall, you will need to cut back shoots to prevent them clogging up guttering and growing across windows.

■ **Virginia creeper** Another popular climber for clothing house walls is the Virginia creeper *(Parthenocissus quinquefolia)*. This can be cut back hard in winter or summer if the need arises. While not quite so rampant, *Parthenocissus henryana* will also need to be kept in check.

JASMINE

When first planted, strong growth from the base of winter-flowering jasmine *(Jasminum nudiflorum)* can be encouraged by cutting back young shoots by up to two-thirds of their length. As they develop, tie in new shoots evenly across the support to create a framework of branches.

Immediately after flowering, in late winter or early spring, remove some of the dead flowering shoots. Not only will this make the plant look tidier, but it will also prevent a build-up of dead wood on which pests and diseases might take hold. More importantly, it will also stimulate the development of otherwise dormant buds, which will burst into leafy growth and new flowering shoots for the following season. Use pruning shears to thin the flowered shoots by one-third,

but take care not to remove any that have not yet flowered. If you thin as soon as the current season's flowers fade, there is less risk of removing any of the new leafy shoots, which would curtail next season's flowering. At the same time, remove any dead, weak, and crossing stems and continue to tie in new shoots to fill any gaps. Prune back vigorous stems to a pair of buds to encourage side stems to grow. Reduce sideshoots back to a pair of buds to stimulate new shoots.

Watch out for any trailing stems. These will root themselves if they touch the ground. Either remove them if not needed or tie them in to the support. If an established plant becomes overgrown, cut it back hard. New growth will be vigorous although flowering may take several years to resume fully.

4

WHEN TO PRUNE OTHER CLIMBERS

AFTER FLOWERING

Akebia quinata
Chocolate vine
Jasminum mesnyi
Primrose jasmine
Trachelospermum jasminoides
Star jasmine

WHEN DORMANT, WINTER/EARLY SPRING
Actinidia kolomikta
Kolomikta vine
 Allemanda carthartica
Golden trumpet
Billardiera longiflora
Climbing blueberry, purple apple berry
Clerodendrum bungei
Glory flower
Eccremocarpus scaber
Chilean glory flower
Humulus lupulus 'Aureus'
Golden hop

Ipomoea lobata
Spanish flag
Ipomoea quamoclit
Star glory
Jasminum officinale
Summer jasmine
Lapageria rosea
Chilean bellflower
Mandevilla laxa
Chilean jasmine
Passiflora
Passionflower
Plumbago capensis
Cape leadwort
Solanum crispum
Chilean potato tree
Solanum jasminoides
Potato vine
Vitis coignetiae
Crimson glory vine

PASSIONFLOWER

IVIES

Ivies (*Hedera* spp.) need no specific pruning. On young plants, remove any weak-looking shoots to encourage stronger growth. Once established, ivies require cutting back periodically to keep them in check. On variegated climbers, such as *Hedera helix* 'Tricolor,' keep an eye out for shoots that have reverted to plain green, and cut these out as soon as you spot them (see pp. 8–9).

CLIMBING COMBINATION
Growing two climbers together on a wall or fence can be rewarding. Here, a white clematis contrasts with *Solanum crispum* 'Glasnevin.'

4

GROWING ON WALLS AND FENCES

Flowering climbers grown against a wall or fence will need some careful pruning and training in the early stages to build up a strong framework of shoots that will cover the surface evenly. After that has been achieved, most will only need regular deadheading and cutting back of some of the longer growths to keep them looking good.

In addition to clematis, honeysuckle, roses, and wisteria, there are a few other flowering climbers that can be used to clothe a wall or fence.

Actinidia kolomikta
Kolomikta vine
Best grown in a sunny site, this twining climber is valued for its heart-shaped leaves which have splashes of white or pink. In early spring, prune new plants hard to encourage a strong framework of stems. Once established, prune only if necessary.

Berberidopsis corallina
Coral plant
Evergreen, woody-stemmed climber with clusters of globular, deep red flowers in late summer. Train to shape. Cut out dead growth in spring.

Campsis radicans
Common trumpet creeper
A vigorous, deciduous, self-clinging climber with long, trumpet-shaped scarlet flowers from late summer to fall. Shorten sideshoots to three or four buds in early spring. Overgrown plants respond well to hard pruning.

Chaenomeles
Japanese quince
Ideal for clothing a cold, windy east- or north-facing wall or fence. *C. speciosa* 'Moerloosei' has pink and white spring flowers, *C. s.* 'Vivalis' is pure white, while *C* x *superba* 'Rowalene' is crimson. Once the basic framework is formed, spur-prune sideshoots back to three or four buds.

Hydrangea petiolaris
Climbing hydrangea
Deciduous self-clinging climber with lacy heads of small white flowers in summer. Deadhead and cut back overlong growths after flowering.

Passiflora
Passionflower
Woody-stemmed tendril climber with exotic flowers followed by egg-shaped fruit. Provide wires, and thin out crowded growth in spring.

Pileostegia viburnoides
Slow-growing self-clinging evergreen, with tiny white or cream flowers in late summer. Prune in spring if needed.

Schizophragma integrifolium
Deciduous aerial-root climber bearing white summer flowers in flat heads. Tie young plants to a support. Prune in spring, but only if necessary.

ACTINIDIA KOLOMIKTA

4

FRUIT TREES AND BUSHES

Pruning is vital when it comes to fruit. If you want your trees and bushes to become, and then remain, productive, knowing how and when to prune is very important. The most complex fruit trees to prune are apples and pears, not because the pruning itself is difficult but because these two fruits can be grown in many different ways. Standard trees, smaller trained bushes, cordons, and espaliers all have their own distinct needs. Next come the other tree fruits such as plums, cherries, peaches, apricots, and figs, while mulberries and quinces need very little attention.

The easiest fruits to prune are cane fruits, namely raspberries, blackberries, and the various hybrid berries such as loganberries. Black, red, and white currants and blueberries need a little more thought, while grapevines have their own set of pruning rules.

5

PRUNING FRUIT

$\mathbf{B}$oth top fruit, such as apples and pears, and most soft fruit, such
as currants and raspberries, need careful and regular pruning to
keep them in good condition, healthy, and productive. Pruning is
best performed annually, either when the plant is dormant during
the winter months or in the summer after cropping is complete.

WHY PRUNE?

Pruning encourages new shoots to
grow: the harder a branch is cut
back, the more vigorous the new
growth will be. During the first
few years, the aim of pruning is to
establish a basic framework, building
a strong, large plant as quickly as
possible. Once established, a different
pruning regime will encourage a
good crop of fruit each year.

Initial pruning and training aims
to: develop a particular shape, be it
bush, cordon, or fan, for example; to
keep branches and stems well spaced
to allow in light, air, and sun to ripen
the wood and fruit; to encourage
fruit to form by removing unwanted
growth shoots but leaving fruit buds;
and to remove all weak, dead, and
diseased wood.

FRUITING RED CURRANT
Correct pruning will ensure that you achieve
good results. This red currant is bushy and
healthy and producing an excellent crop of fruit.

THE BEST TIME TO PRUNE SOFT FRUIT

Blackberries	In fall after fruiting
Black currants	Late fall or early winter
Blueberries	Early spring
Gooseberries	In winter while dormant
Gooseberry cordons	Summer and winter
Raspberries, summer-fruiting	In summer after fruiting
Raspberries, fall-fruiting	Late winter
Red and white currants	In winter while dormant
Red and white currant cordons	Summer and winter

5

PRUNING SOFT FRUIT

All woody soft fruits, except fall-fruiting raspberries, produce on stems that are at least one year old. There are two main pruning periods (see also panel on p. 72). Winter pruning improves the shape of a plant, while summer pruning restricts growth and maintains form. Always dip the pruning shears in disinfectant before pruning each plant.

PRUNING TREE FRUIT

■ **When to prune** Fruit trees are usually pruned in late winter or early spring, when they are still dormant. Prune hard at this time and again, lightly, in fall (see also panel below). Established free-standing apple, pear, and plum trees can be largely left alone, apart from removing diseased, crossing, weak, or unwanted branches. Do this in winter for apples and pears (pip fruit) or summer for plums (stone fruit).

■ **Training to shape** Fruit trees can be pruned and trained into a variety of forms, the most natural being a freestanding, compact tree known, confusingly, as a bush. Apples, pears, and plums can all be grown in this fashion. The other forms, such as cordons, espaliers, and fans, are discussed in detail later in this chapter, because they all require a slightly different pruning routine.

■ **How to prune** First take out dead, damaged, or diseased branches (when removing diseased limbs, disinfect the pruning tool before making the next cut to prevent the spread of disease). Then remove crossing or crowded branches. If established trees are too productive, weighing down branches with large quantities of undersized fruit, remove some of the fruit buds in spring. Fruit buds are normally fatter and more rounded than an ordinary growth bud.

THE BEST TIME TO PRUNE TREE FRUIT		
Apples	Bush trees	Winter or early spring
	Trained trees	Summer
Apricots	All forms	Late summer after fruiting
Cherries	All forms	Midsummer after fruiting
Figs		Spring and summer
Peaches and nectarines	All forms	Midsummer, after fruiting
Pears	Bush trees	Winter or early spring
	Trained trees	Mid- or late summer
Plums	Bush trees	Midsummer
	Trained trees	Midsummer

5

APPLE AND PEAR TREES

Both apple and pear trees are available in several sizes and trained forms. Taller-growing standards, half-standards, and more compact bush trees are all more or less the same thing, having several branches on top of a clear main trunk. These are all forms that are easy to train and maintain, but picking fruit will be more difficult from the taller trees. The bush form, which is grown on a trunk just 2–3ft (60–90cm) high, is better suited to today's smaller gardens.

TRAINING APPLES AND PEARS

■ **Espaliers, cordons, and fans**
Apples and pears can be trained as espaliers, which have a few pairs of evenly spaced horizontal branches coming from a central vertical stem. Grown in this fashion, supported by posts and wires, they make an attractive divider between different parts of the garden, taking up less space than a hedge. Taking up even less space, and making good use of an otherwise unproductive area, against walls or fences, apples can be trained as

cordons (single stems trained at an angle, usually 45°), while both apples and pears can be fan-trained against a wall, where the added warmth and protection will help fruit ripen.

■ **Arches and "stepovers"** Some fruit trees can also be trained over arches to form a fruiting arbor or tunnel. "Stepover" apple trees are a new idea, where the tree is trained horizontally just above ground level on a system of posts and wires.

PLANTING AND INITIAL PRUNING

Apples and pears are pruned in much the same way, although pears should be pruned less heavily in their early years. Much will depend on the age of the tree when you plant it (see below). Before planting any fruit tree, cut off cleanly any damaged or diseased branches and roots.

■ **Selecting a tree** Maiden – or one-year-old – fruit trees consist of a single stem and will require the most attention when it comes to initial pruning and training. Two-year-old trees will be partly trained, but a three- or four-year-old tree with a well-established crown, although costing more, will need less attention and will crop much sooner.

5

ROOTSTOCKS

Each fruit tree is grafted onto a rootstock, and it is this that governs a tree's vigor and eventual size. Rootstocks are coded: M27 is a dwarfing rootstock, while the most vigorous is MM11. Some cherries are grafted onto a dwarfing rootstock called Colt, which is ideal for fan-training. When buying, take note of the rootstock to ensure that it suits both the chosen location and the form the tree will take. When planting a grafted tree, do not plant it too deep. The graft union, where the rootstock joins the stem, should be above the soil.

FORMATIVE PRUNING

Late fall is the optimum time to buy and plant fruit trees. You can then begin formative pruning in winter or early spring. Starting with a maiden tree, the aim is to encourage a straight trunk that will support a bowl-shaped system of branches growing upward and outward, and that also allows light and air into the center.

Always prune branches back to a healthy looking bud. This will stimulate sideshoots to form along the branch. Choose a bud that points in an outward direction so that the resulting shoot will also grow outward, keeping the center of the tree open and balanced.

For the same reason, you should remove any shoots that are growing downward or toward the center of the tree, as well as any branches that are damaged, dead, or diseased.

■ **First winter, after planting** Cut the central stem (leader) back to a strong branch, leaving three or more well-placed, outward-growing, healthy branches just below the cut. These will be the main branches. Shorten them by two-thirds of their length.

■ **Second winter** Prune back the main branches by half, cutting to an outward-facing bud. Remove any sideshoots growing too low or crossing others, then prune back those that are left to about one-third of their original length.

■ **Third winter** On trees that bear spurs (fruiting sideshoots), shorten the previous season's growth on the main branches by a quarter to a half. Shorten sideshoots to four to six buds, removing weak or damaged ones. On tip-bearing trees (fruiting at the main tips), only prune badly placed or crossing sideshoots. The next spring, do not let fruit form to allow branches and sideshoots to grow stronger. Rub off embryo fruits after the blossom has fallen.

5

1 In the first winter after planting, prune the central stem back to a strong shoot. There should be three or four outward-facing sideshoots below the cut. Shorten these by two-thirds.

2 In the second winter, select a few shoots to be the main branches, and reduce them by half. Prune others to one-third of their original length, and remove any unwanted shoots.

PRUNING AN ESTABLISHED TREE

Most kinds of apple and pear trees produce fruit on short, woody spurs borne on branches that are three years old. So, to prune an established tree effectively, you will need to be able to tell how old each branch is.

Look at the tree after it has shed its leaves. A one-year-old shoot has small growth buds lying close to the branch. These shoots should not be pruned. Shoots showing fatter fruit buds appear on branches that are

two years old, and any weak ones should be cut back to two buds. Leave more buds on any strong two-year-old shoots. In their third year, branches have developed fruit spurs. Prune some of these back to one spur to encourage replacement growth.

Some apple trees, such as 'Bramley Seedling,' bear fruit on the tips of their sideshoots as well as on fruiting spurs. These do not need so much pruning.

SPUR-BEARERS
In winter, prune mature spur-bearing trees by removing dead and diseased branches, thinning congested spurs, shortening weak main shoots by a half and strong ones by a quarter, and cutting back older branches.

5

TIP-BEARERS
In winter, remove all dead, diseased, and damaged growth from established tip-bearing trees, cut back older fruited wood to a young shoot, and tip-prune the main branches to encourage the production of replacement growth.

PRUNING SPUR-BEARING TREES

For apple and pear trees that bear fruit on spurs, in winter remove dead and diseased wood and any crossing or badly placed branches (see p. 76). Shorten or thin congested spurs. Also shorten any weak main branches by about half their length, but stronger ones should be cut back by no more than a quarter. Cut back any older branches that are forming the main framework of the tree to leave about 12in (30cm) between them.

APPLES BORNE ON A SPUR
This healthy looking cluster of apples has been produced on a spur, or short fruiting sideshoot coming off a main branch of the tree. You will need to prune this type of fruit tree differently from the tip-bearing kind (see below) in order to stimulate a good crop.

PRUNING TIP-BEARING TREES

For trees that bear fruit at shoot tips, in winter remove dead, diseased, and overcrowded branches. Cut back older fruited wood to a young shoot or basal bud. Prune the tips of main branches, or they may snap. Remove old, large branches from the center.

APPLES PRODUCED AT THE TIP
This is an example of an apple tree that bears fruit right at the tips of its branches rather than on short spurs (see above). In this case, pruning involves cutting back old fruited branches to stimulate healthy, strong new shoots to grow.

THE RIGHT CUT

When removing a branch or shoot, always cut back to another branch or shoot, taking care not to leave a snag. When shortening a shoot, make the cut immediately above a bud, but not so close as to risk damaging the bud.

5

CORDONS

Apples and pears, except tip-bearers, can both be grown as a cordon with one main stem grown at an angle. If the layout of your garden allows, cordons should be planted with their stems pointing north. This exposes the trees to as much sunshine as possible.

■ **First winter** Plant the young trees at an angle of 45°. This is easier if you tie a bamboo cane to the support wires at that angle and then tie the leader, or main stem, to the cane. Shorten any laterals over 4in (10cm) long to three buds. Do not prune the main stem.

■ **First summer** At the end of the growing season, prune new laterals from the main stem back to a few leaves above the basal cluster of leaves (a ring of leaves at the base of each shoot). Sublaterals will have formed on the existing sideshoots.

Cut these back to two leaves. This will encourage fruiting spurs to form.

■ **Second winter** You can now prune the leader each winter. How much you cut off depends on how quickly the cordon is growing. If little growth has been made, prune hard; if the plant is well established and growing strongly, just cut the tips back. Make the cut above a bud on opposite sides of the branch, so the leader grows as straight as possible. When it reaches the top wire, cut back the new growth, pruning above a bud or new shoot.

■ **Routine summer pruning** Prune all trained trees in summer to restrict growth and encourage the formation of fruit buds. Cut back lateral shoots longer than 8in (20cm) to within three or four leaves above their basal leaf clusters. Trim the sublaterals to one or two leaves.

5

PEAR CORDONS
Apples and pears grown in this way help you maximize their fruiting potential, while taking up less space than a normal tree. The fruits are also easier to harvest.

REJUVENATING A NEGLECTED APPLE OR PEAR TREE

This renovation should be carried out over a couple of years, pruning in winter. The aim is to open up the center of the tree and remove wood that is no longer productive, so you end up with evenly spaced branches radiating from the crown.

■ **Dead wood** Cut any dead wood right back to areas of vigorous growth. Also remove any wood infected with canker. Small, weak branches can be pruned away completely, while larger branches should be cut back to healthy wood.

■ **Congestion** Overcrowded branches lead to congestion which will encourage disease. Prune to open up the center of the tree. Work out from the center to leave four or five thick, evenly spaced main branches.

■ **Crossing branches** These will block light and air needed to ripen the young wood, and they may also rub against other branches. Remove them, cutting back to their point of origin or to a strong sideshoot.

■ **Weak branches** Take out any weak or spindly branches, either cut out altogether or take back to a vigorous shoot. Thin overcrowded spurs and encourage sideshoots to develop from lower on the branches by cutting them back by one-third to a half, cutting to an outward-facing bud.

■ **Mulch and feed** After such drastic pruning, give the tree a thick mulch of well-rotted manure or garden compost. If the tree is growing in a lawn, apply a general fertilizer in the form of granules and water well.

■ **Thinning spurs** After five or six years, in winter, cut some of the overcrowded spurs back flush with the main stem. As young shoots grow in their place, rub some off to leave the rest well spaced. In summer, prune back to three or four buds.

OLD APPLE TREE
This mature apple tree has provided good service for many years, but would now benefit greatly from a program of rejuvenative pruning to give it a new lease on life.

5

ESPALIERS

Apples and pears can also be grown as espaliers, where the branches are trained to grow horizontally along a system of parallel wires. You can save yourself a lot of effort, however, if you buy a three- or four-year-old tree that has already been started as an espalier. It should begin to bear fruit within a couple of years.

■ **Initial training** To train a tree yourself, look for a two-year-old tree which has two nearly opposing laterals low down on a vertical leader, or main stem. After planting, tie these two horizontal shoots to the bottom wire, 18in (45cm) above the ground, to form the espalier's lowest pair of branches. Then cut the central stem, or leader, back to a strong bud, 2–3in (5–7.5cm) above the next wire, 15in (37cm) above the bottom one.

■ **Subsequent training** During the growing season, a number of new shoots will grow from the leader. Choose two opposing sideshoots closest to the second wire, and tie them to it. You may need to tie these to canes, and slowly lower them down to the wire in order to train them horizontally. Remove the canes when the branches are growing away strongly in the right direction.

Prune sideshoots on lower branches back to three or four leaves of the basal cluster and shorten other laterals on the leader by two-thirds. Then continue to build up tiers until the tree reaches the desired size.

APPLE ESPALIER
After several years, your espalier apple tree should look like this, with a number of well-spaced, productive, horizontal-growing laterals.

5

1 In summer, on established espaliers, take all new sideshoots back to three or four leaves from the base.

2 At the same time, cut out completely any shoots growing vigorously in a vertical direction from either the main stem or the horizontal ones.

■ **Pruning established espaliers**
In summer, cut all new laterals from the main framework of branches back to three or four leaves above the basal cluster to create fruiting spurs. Reduce sublaterals to one leaf. Any vigorous upright shoots growing from either the main stem or the horizontal branches need to be removed completely.

Spurs that have borne fruit should be cut back by at least one-third of their length in winter to encourage the formation of the growth buds which will form next year's new shoots. Cut these shoots back the following year in late summer to form new fruiting spurs.

POOR PEAR CROP

• If a pear tree fails to fruit well, and a late frost or cold spring winds are not to blame, it could be that the tree is overcrowded. If this is the case, the tree needs to be cut back extremely hard, removing all overcrowded and congested branches.

• Pear trees also tend to produce an abundance of fruiting spurs. Too many of these will sap the tree's energy and reduce its cropping potential, so you should always remember to thin these out in midsummer.

5

OTHER FRUIT TREES

As well as apples and pears, popular tree fruits include plums, peaches, nectarines, apricots, and cherries, although some of these require a certain degree of warmth in order to thrive. These can also be grown in a number of different ways, including fan-training.

PLUMS

Plums can be grown as a standard, cordon, or espalier (as previously described) or as a fan (see p. 84). Once the main framework of branches has been formed after four or five years, annual pruning is simply removing dead, diseased, and damaged shoots and branches. Also remove some older branches to let light and air into the center.

SUPPORTING BRANCHES

Plum wood is more brittle than most, and branches on older trees are prone to breaking under the weight of fruit. You should always prop up any broken branch, rather than removing it, because removal will result in the growth of new leaf shoots instead of new fruit.

■ **Silver leaf disease** Unlike other top fruit, plums should always be pruned in spring or early summer and never in fall or winter. The reason for this is a disease called silver leaf, an often fatal fungal infection which can enter a plum tree through cut surfaces. The spores are about from midsummer until the end of winter, and so, by avoiding any pruning during this period, the chance of infection is greatly reduced. If silver leaf does strike, you will find a silvery sheen on some leaves. Cut out and burn any infected branches. Be sure to cut right back to sound wood; diseased wood will have a brown stain through it. If only one or two branches have been infected, the tree is worth saving. If more than one-third of the tree is infected, the only option is to fell the tree as there is no chemical cure for silver leaf.

■ **Suckers** Plum trees also tend to produce suckers from the roots, and these should be pulled away as soon as they are spotted (see p. 54).

PLUM TREE IN BLOSSOM
As well as providing a rich crop of fruit later in the season, fruit trees like this plum serve up a delightful display of flowers in the spring.

5

PEACHES, NECTARINES, AND APRICOTS

Although in frost-prone climates peaches, nectarines, and apricots prefer the shelter of a greenhouse, in warmer areas they can be fan-trained against a sunny wall. Basic fan-training is similar to that described later (see p. 84), but delay cutting back the main stem until late spring, when all danger of frost is past. The two sideshoots chosen for the base of the fan should be about 9in (23cm) above the ground.

Peaches and nectarines fruit on the previous season's growth, so three years after planting you can allow fruiting shoots to form. These should be spaced along the main stems at 6-in (15-cm) intervals, pinching out all the others. At the end of summer, tie these in to the supporting wires, nipping out the tips of any that are longer than 18in (45cm).

The following spring, remove any shoots that are growing in toward the wall or away from it, and cut remaining shoots back to four or six leaves. At the same time, thin out the developing fruit, leaving about 9in (23cm) between them. Once they have cropped, cut back all fruited shoots to the cluster of buds at their base. As the new shoots grow, tie them into the support wires at an even spacing. At the same time, cut out dead and diseased material and all surplus and overcrowded wood.

Apricots are prone to dieback, so check trees regularly, removing any dead wood and discolored shoots.

FAN-TRAINED PEACH
A peach tree trained as a fan against a sunny, warm, sheltered wall like this one should turn out to be healthy and productive.

5

CHERRIES

Since the introduction of the dwarf Colt rootstock, cherries have become a realistic proposition, even in the smallest of gardens, where they can be fan-trained against a wall (net the fruit to keep the birds off), or grown as an espalier. Where space allows, you can also grow them as a 12-ft (3.5-m) bush.

■ **Pruning cherries** An established cherry tree requires minimal pruning: just shorten or thin branches where necessary to avoid overcrowding, and keep the tree healthy by removing dead, diseased, and damaged wood. If you are growing the acid cherry, 'Morello,' then, after the fruit has been picked, remove some of less productive branches in order to stimulate new growth.

INITIAL FAN-TRAINING
To start a cherry (here 'Morello') into a fan shape, cut back the leader to just above two nearly opposite laterals in early summer. The laterals can later be tied in to the canes.

WHY FAN-TRAIN?

Fan-training against a wall or a fence is a productive way to grow fruit trees such as cherries, apricots, peaches, and nectarines, as well as apples, pears, and plums, particularly in today's smaller gardens. Protected by the shelter of a wall or fence, they will crop more heavily in cooler climates, while in warmer areas they can also be grown on canes and wires in the open garden. You can start either with a feathered maiden (a one-year-old tree with several well-placed sideshoots) or a partially trained fan, which although a little more expensive to buy will save you time and effort. Once the basic fan shape has been formed (see below), your tree will start to produce fruits by the fourth year. Routine pruning will then be all that is required, cutting out fruited wood and tying in new shoots.

After 10 years, a fan-trained tree will reach a height of up to 8ft (2.4m) and a spread of about 6m (20ft).

HOW TO FAN-TRAIN A FRUIT TREE

5

■ **Stage 1** Plant a tree in late fall to midwinter. In early spring, prune the main stem (leader) to about 24in (60cm) above the ground.

■ **Stage 2** In early summer, choose two laterals roughly opposite to each other and about 12in (30cm) above

the ground to form the base of the fan. Cut the leader back to just above these sideshoots, to leave a Y-shape (see picture above).

■ **Stage 3** When these sideshoots are 16–18in (40–45cm) long, tie them to canes at 45° to the leader, and then attach the canes to the horizontal support wires. Early in the following spring, you should once more reduce these two (by now) side branches to 16–18in (40–45cm).

■ **Stage 4** Choose four well-placed shoots on each of the two side branches. Aim for two shoots growing up, one pointing down, and one extending from the top bud. These will form the main "ribs" of the fan. Tie them to the support wires as they grow.

■ **Stage 5** Early the following spring, cut back each of these eight shoots to an upward-facing bud, leaving them about 30in (75cm) long.

■ **Stage 6** As new shoots form, either tie them in or remove them if they are not wanted. Generally, shoots growing parallel to the wall should be kept, and those growing toward or away from the wall should be removed. Thin those that are left in spring to leave 4in (10cm) between them. Remove all growth below the lowest support wire.

■ **Stage 7** To encourage fruiting, pinch out the tips of the shoots in summer once they have five or six leaves. Then, at the end of the growing season, shorten them back to three buds.

■ **Stage 8** Once a branch has filled its allotted space, cut it back to a healthy sideshoot.

FAN-TRAINED PLUM TREE
This plum has been trained as a fan along a system of wires, rather than a wall or fence, to create a perfectly symmetrical shape.

5

FIGS

It is preferable to grow figs against a sunny wall, with their vigorous roots contained in a pot. As young shoots grow, figs will develop at the base of each leaf. In frost-prone areas, these fruit will not ripen outside in the same year; and, although they will grow quite large, they will not survive the winter and so should be removed in early fall.

■ **Initial pruning and training** Figs need very little pruning in their early years. As they grow, shoots should be tied in, in a fan shape, leaving about 12in (30cm) between the branches. Remove any surplus growth to allow the sun in to ripen the wood.

■ **Restricting roots** If the vigorous root growth of a fig tree is likely to cause problems in your garden, plant it in a 15-in (38-cm) container to restrict the roots, and train the branches against a wall.

■ **Pruning fig trees**
Prune established fig trees during the middle of spring, when you can be certain that all threat of frost has passed. First cut out any wood that has been damaged by ice or frost. Leave enough branches and shoots to cover the wall, then thin surplus branches by cutting them back to a lower branch or removing them completely at ground level. In early summer, if young shoots are pinched back to five leaves new fruiting shoots will form.

Later it may be necessary to thin any excessive growth that is shading fruiting branches, but always remember to leave enough shoots to carry the following year's fruit.

■ **Suckers** Any suckers that appear along the trunk can be tied in as they are not a threat. Fig cultivars are grown from cuttings produced by their own rootstock, rather than grafted on to other rootstocks.

Warning

It is the little embryo figs that form in leaf axils toward the tip of a shoot which, if they survive the winter, will start to swell the following spring and crop in midsummer. So, when pruning, take care not to cut off the tips of the shoots that are carrying fruit.

POT-GROWN FIG

5

MULBERRIES AND QUINCES

Both mulberries and quinces grow to fairly substantial proportions and are only really suitable for large gardens. In addition, they usually only crop well in warmer, drier climates. They are worth growing anyway because they can be a decorative feature in their own right, each having gnarled branches. The quince has pretty pale pink or white spring blossom and yellow fruits in fall, and a quince tree can also be trained against a wall.

■ **Mulberries** Only prune these if absolutely necessary, as mulberry branches bleed when cut. Once the main framework has been established, you can shorten some of the young shoots in summer to encourage fruiting spurs to form.

Remove any dead, damaged, or crossing branches soon after the leaves have fallen.

■ **Quinces** These also need little pruning, although as the tree matures its growth becomes untidy and often overcrowded. During the early years, reduce half the previous year's growth on the sideshoots by about half its length, and keep the center of the tree as open as possible. This lets in light and allows air to circulate.

Once the main framework is established, remove any dead, damaged, or overcrowded branches in winter. Thin out congested fruiting spurs and remove any suckers that emerge along the trunk or at its base.

MULBERRY TREE
This healthy young specimen has not yet reached its final size. Mulberry trees can eventually attain 20ft (6m) in both height and spread.

5

SOFT FRUIT

There are three types of soft fruit: bush fruit, cane fruit, and strawberries. It is only the first two types that need any serious pruning, as strawberries are not woody plants. Soft-fruit, or berry, bushes need good formative pruning if they are to stay healthy and productive, while fruiting canes need careful training and support.

BLACK CURRANTS

Black currants form multi-stemmed bushes, fruiting best on one-year-old branches. To establish a multi-stemmed bush and stimulate plenty of new shoots, pruning in the first year has to be drastic. After planting in late fall, cut all the shoots down to just one bud above soil level, cutting directly above the bud. The following winter, cut back any weak, inward- or downward-facing shoots as close to the ground as possible. Leave six to eight strong new shoots to shape the bush.

Thin established bushes each year during a mild spell in late fall or winter. You can prune after picking the fruit, but it is easier if you wait until the leaves have dropped.

PLANTING SOFT FRUIT

Always plant one-year-old bushes. Once established, berry bushes need regular and careful pruning if they are to continue to fruit well.

Take about a third of the old, dark, fruited wood back to the base to maintain an open bush that lets in light and air. Also prune out any low-growing branches and remove crowded, crossing, and weak shoots.

5

PLANTING BLACK CURRANTS
These plants are one year old, and after planting will need to be pruned hard in order to stimulate new shoots from near to ground level. These will form the fruiting stems in the following year.

GOOSEBERRIES AND RED AND WHITE CURRANTS

Gooseberries and red and white currants are usually grown as single-stemmed bushes. Their shoots form an open-centered bush growing from a short, central stem. Where space is limited, currants can also be grown as a fan or cordon against a wall or fence, while gooseberries can be trained as a cordon.

Red and white currants fruit on wood that is at least two years old, while gooseberries produce fruit on both previous season's wood and spurs on older wood. Pruning is the same for all three.

After planting, to create a clear, single stem, pull off any suckers and cut back to the base any branches less than 6–9in (15–23cm) above the old soil mark on the stem. Prune the remaining framework of branches by about a half to three-quarters of their length, by cutting to an outward-facing bud. If this has already been done by the supplier, just trim the shoots by about 1in (2.5cm).

Thereafter, routine pruning (in winter, but not when the weather is frosty) consists of cutting back new growth on the main stems by about a quarter to a half of their length. Take back sideshoots to within four buds of the main stem.

You may need to remove some of the older branches completely to keep the bush open. This allows light and air into it to ripen the new wood. Always remove dead and diseased wood, as well as any crowded branches in the center.

If summer growth, on dessert gooseberries in particular, is vigorous, new sideshoots can be pruned to within four or five leaves of their base, to prevent excessive foliage shading the ripening fruit.

GOOSEBERRY CORDON
If you have the space, you can try growing gooseberries as a cordon, that is, with a single, upright stem and no main side branches.

MILDEW

Both black currants and gooseberries are prone to the disease powdery mildew. Any shoots showing signs of a white powdery substance should be removed immediately to prevent any spread of the infection.

5

RASPBERRIES

∎ **Summer-fruiting raspberries**
These raspberries produce fruits on their stems, or canes, which have grown from the base of the plant in the previous season. In other words, on wood that is one year old.

Immediately after planting in late fall, cut each cane back to a bud 9–12in (23–30cm) above the soil. As new shoots appear in spring, cut the old cane down to ground level. Pinch out any flowers as they appear, as the canes should not be allowed to crop in their first year. In the following fall, cut out one or two of the weakest canes completely in order to encourage strong new growth. Tie in the remaining canes, which will fruit in the following summer.

Canes that have fruited should be cut down to the ground after harvesting. Also remove any thin, weak, damaged, or diseased canes, retaining about six to nine young,

SUMMER-FRUITING RASPBERRY CANES
Here, the previous season's canes are producing flowers, and the current season's canes are making strong growth for next year's crop.

unfruited canes per plant. Tie these in securely to support wires. Any suckers that develop too far from the main row should be removed.

Tie new canes to support wires as they grow. In a dry summer, surplus growth can be thinned to reduce the plants' demand for water.

∎ **Fall-fruiting raspberries**
Raspberries that fruit in the fall, up until the first frosts, carry their crop on canes that have been produced in the same year. In this case, all the canes should be cut back to ground level toward the end of winter, before any new shoots appear. This also applies to newly planted canes. In the following year, thin the canes in midsummer to leave about half a dozen vigorous stems.

5

BLACKBERRIES, LOGANBERRIES, AND HYBRID BERRIES

Like raspberries, all these berries carry their fruit on canes, which should be cut down to the base after fruiting. Simply cut out all the old, fruited wood, leaving any new growth to fruit the following year. After cutting out the old wood, tie in the new canes to support wires.

In early spring, look out for any frost-damaged tips and prune them back to healthy wood.

Young plants should be cut back to 9–12in (23–30cm) after planting, if this has not already been done. In the spring, wait until shoots appear, then cut away the stumps of the old canes.

OTHER SOFT FRUITS

■ **Strawberries** As these are not woody plants, they do not need any real pruning. However, you will need a sharp knife or pruning shears to cut out any unwanted runners as they appear (see below). After harvesting, cut off the old foliage, to leave about 3–4in (7.5–10cm) of leaf stem above the crown.

CUTTING STRAWBERRY RUNNERS
Unless you want some new plants, remove strawberry runners as soon as you see them. This will concentrate more energy into fruiting.

■ **Blueberries** Leave the plants to establish themselves for a couple of years; then, in early spring, remove twiggy, crossing, or damaged growth. This should encourage a supply of good young shoots, which will then produce fruit on their sideshoots in the following year.

■ **Worcesterberries** These are a hybrid between a gooseberry and a black currant, and they grow like gooseberries; the bushes should be treated similarly (see p. 89).

5

GRAPEVINES

In the case of grapevines, the boundary between what is pruning and what is training is somewhat blurred. What is quite clear, however, is that both training and regular pruning are vital if the plant is to be anything other than a mass of foliage, producing very few grapes.

GROWING GRAPEVINES

The Guyot system (see below) is used for vines grown outside in the open garden. Where space is limited, they are more usually grown as cordons (see p. 93) on a single-rod or rod-and-spur system. The pruning necessary for growing vines in this way is discussed here.

Remember, major pruning of vines should only be carried out in winter (see panel on p. 94), in order to keep sap bleeding to a minimum. You can plant vines in fall or spring under glass, but wait until the weather warms up before planting outdoors. After planting, take the main shoot, called the "rod," down to 18–24in (45–60cm), cutting back to a strong bud on ripe wood near the lowest support wire. Take out all sideshoots and tie the rod to a cane.

GUYOT SYSTEM
This can be used when growing vines in the open garden, and consists of two horizontally trained branches bearing upright fruiting shoots.

5

CREATING A CORDON

Continue to train the main rod up a cane and, as they grow, train laterals along horizontal support wires, at evenly spaced intervals on either side of the main rod. For the first two summers, cut back these laterals to five or six leaves. Any sideshoots that form on the laterals should be taken back to one leaf. Remove all flowers as they appear, as the vine must not be allowed to carry any fruit until its third year.

During a vine's first two winters, shorten the main rod by a half to two-thirds of its length, cutting back to ripe brown wood. Cut back the laterals to about 1in (2.5cm), leaving just one or two buds.

In the third year, when flowers have appeared, cut back what are now fruiting laterals to two leaves beyond the flower cluster. Cut sub-laterals back to just one leaf.

For the sake of the crop, you should allow only one fruiting lateral per spur to develop: you must remove all the others. For the first few years, one bunch of grapes can be allowed to develop on each

GRAPE CORDON
If space is limited, the best way to grow a vine is as a rod-and-spur cordon, in which fruiting sideshoots emanate from a central stem.

lateral; on a more mature grapevine, two or three bunches can be grown.

Thereafter, continue to prune the main rod as described above. Once it reaches the roof, if growing under cover, or the top wire if outside, cut it back to just 1in (2.5cm) beyond the new growth each winter.

ESTABLISHED VINES

As the vine grows older, growth around the sideshoots may become congested, and some of these woody stubs can be sawn off.

By early summer, flower clusters should be visible, and it is these that will develop into bunches of grapes. Pinch out any weak flower clusters, leaving just one well-developed cluster per lateral.

Prune back all laterals that have flower clisters to leave just two leaves beyond the flower cluster. Any laterals without flowers should be cut back to five or six leaves.

5

THINNING FRUIT

When grapevines, or any other fruit tree, set a large, heavy crop, the fruit may need thinning. Tempting as it may be to leave as much fruit on the plant as possible, this will compromise both quality and flavor and excess should be removed.

WHY THIN FRUIT?

The weight of a heavy crop of fruit can split branches. Fruit on young trees should always be thinned, as too heavy a crop in the formative years can restrict the tree's growth and cropping potential. Use pruning shears to remove the central, or "king," fruit in each cluster, and remove any others that are small, damaged, or malformed. Thin out the remaining fruits, leaving them 4–6in (10–15cm) apart. Wait until midsummer, after the drop of freshly set fruitlets, before doing more thinning.

1 Thin grapes down to one bunch per shoot; otherwise there will not be enough room for each bunch to develop properly.

2 To create larger grapes, thin out some individual fruits within a bunch as they develop, using pruning shears or scissors designed for the job.

ROUTINE PRUNING OF GRAPEVINES

WINTER

• Cut the main stem, or rod, back to two buds of new growth each year.

• In midwinter, untie the rod and bend it over horizontally. This will encourage an even flow of sap, and shoots will develop further down the rod. Retie the rod on the vertical in early spring when buds start to break.

• Cut laterals back to the first strong bud.

SUMMER

• Prune back all laterals without any flower clusters to about five or six leaves.

• Cut back all fruiting laterals to two leaves beyond the developing grape bunch.

• Pinch out the weakest flower clusters so that the plant can concentrate its energies on fewer, but larger, bunches of grapes.

5

SPECIAL PROJECTS

Some pruning techniques have been developed to achieve certain special effects, either for ornamental purposes or for the sake of a plant's health and productivity. For example, a particular type of pruning is needed when plants are grown over a pergola, arch, or other garden structure. The art of topiary is another special pruning technique, demanding time and patience; as in bonsai, where stems, branches, and roots all have their own pruning requirements.

Training a standard fuchsia involves a different kind of pruning regime, while two giants of the border, bamboo and pampas grass, need an annual overhaul.

Inside the home and conservatory, houseplants can be given a helping hand to look and perform better. Out in the kitchen garden, some edible crops can be encouraged to maximize their yield with a little judicial pruning.

TRAINING PLANTS

P ergolas, arches, and other structures such as obelisks and tripods
(see p. 62) can provide an effective support for many plants, and
create a dramatic focal point when draped with just a single species,
such as delicate wisteria, golden laburnum, or a scented climbing rose.

USING A FRAMEWORK

Climbers need careful training if they
are to grow over the entire support.
As new stems appear, tie them in
loosely, remembering that most
climbers flower better if shoots are
trained horizontally. With climbing
and rambling roses, encourage
flowering shoots to form near the
base by spiraling the main shoots
around the support's uprights when
growth is still young and flexible.
Clematis montana and wisteria also
respond to this treatment. Always tie

in shoots gently with soft twine,
and allow room for growth and
movement. In spring or late summer,
remove dead, damaged, and diseased
wood, pruning the main stems to
encourage new sideshoots to form.
When the main shoots reach the
top, prune them back.

GOLDEN LABURNUM ARCH
Although laburnum is not a climber, it can
be trained to grow over an arch (see panel
on p. 97) and produce this wonderful effect.

6

TRAINING WISTERIA OVER A PERGOLA

A pergola is a horizontal framework supported on posts that can form a colorful covered walkway when draped with flowering climbers such as wisteria. It will probably take several years of careful training to cover the structure, but the eventual rewards will be well worth the effort.

1 Tie in young, pliable shoots regularly to form an even covering over the support. Shoots that are tied horizontally will flower more profusely than those that are tied in vertically.

2 Prune back or carefully tie in any stems that are hanging down.

LABURNUM ARCH

• Plant one- or two-year-old saplings at 8-ft (2.4-m) intervals.

• In early spring, train the supple new growth up and over a metal arch.

• To encourage more sideshoots, lightly prune back the main stem.

• As plants become dormant each year, prune sideshoots to within two or three buds of the main framework of branches to encourage flowering.

3 Cut back non-essential main stems by about one-third in late summer. Also prune then to encourage the production of more shoots and flowers (see p. 67). In winter, shorten these shoots again to two buds.

6

ROSE OBELISK OR TRIPOD

Where space is restricted, an eye-catching display can be achieved by training one of the less vigorous climbing roses up an obelisk or tripod. Suitable roses include 'Bantry Bay' and 'American Pillar,' as well as miniature climbing roses that reach just 6ft (2m) or so high.

To do this, plant a rose 10in (25cm) away from the base of each leg of the support. Once the plants have reached the top of the structure, cut any wayward shoots back to a bud just below the top. Prune flowered shoots back to a low, outward-facing bud. Cut crowded older stems right back to newer growth. Remove any older growth completely. Train new stems at ground level to cover gaps lower down the structure, spiraling them around the tripod's legs.

VERTICAL INTEREST
This feature, using the rose 'Bantry Bay,' provides some welcome height in a border of low-growing plants.
The support can be a preformed metal structure, as here, or a simple rustic-pole tripod construction, but it must be about 8–10ft (2.4–3m) high.

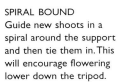

SPIRAL BOUND
Guide new shoots in a spiral around the support and then tie them in. This will encourage flowering lower down the tripod.

6

ROSE SWAG

Often seen in display gardens at the great horticultural shows, a rose swag is a decorative feature that also lends itself to the domestic garden. Climbing or rambling roses with pliable stems are trained around a thick rope suspended between 8-ft (2.4-m) posts. Choose a really fragrant rose, like 'Félicité Perpétue' or 'Bobbie James,' and the result will be even more pleasing.

Plant a suitable rose 12in (30cm) from the base of each post, and let it grow to the top. Prune according to rose type (see Chapter 3).

Once the rose has become firmly established, pruning is a little more tricky, as crowded stems will need thinning. Wearing heavy-duty gloves, try to unravel as much of the rose as possible from the rope and prune vigorous flowered stems back to a new healthy shoot. Try to retain any shoots that are growing in the direction of the rope.

ROSA GENTILIANA
The abundant clusters of rose blooms on this swag make a superb feature for any garden, not just those that are created for display purposes.

6

CREATING SHAPES WITH TOPIARY

Another special pruning technique is topiary, the art of clipping and training evergreen shrubs and plants into special shapes such as cones, spirals, and lollipops. Bay, box, privet, and yew are traditionally used, but there are other shrubs that can be clipped into geometric living ornaments for the garden.

Simple shapes can be fashioned from mature shrubs, but more complex ones, such as birds and animals, need to be started from scratch from a young plant. Remember: the simpler the shape, the easier it will be to maintain. Rounded and free-form shapes are easier to achieve than precise edges and geometric forms. Let the growth of the plant guide your choice. Box *(Buxus sempervirens)* and yew *(Taxus baccata)* are generally used for large pieces, while *Buxus sempervirens* 'Suffruticosa' lends itself to smaller, more complex shapes and box edging. You will get quicker results with privet *(Ligustrum ovalifolium)* or small-leaved ivies *(Hedera)*.

■ **Shaping the plant** You can use canes tied together as a guide for geometric shapes, such as cones or pyramids. More elaborate shapes, such as spheres or spirals, animals and birds, can be fashioned from chicken wire or a wire frame, which is placed over the plant to act as a guide. The frame will be hidden by foliage after a few years.

■ **Trimming** The first trim needs to be given straight after planting. Then, to keep it looking immaculate, topiary needs to be trimmed with an electric hedge trimmer or really sharp hand or topiary shears two or three times a year. You may get away with a single summer trim, but topiary will soon become misshapen if not regularly trimmed. Regular clipping every few weeks in the summer will be necessary in the first few years to form the shape, and some shoots will need to be tied in with soft twine to help them grow in the right direction.

■ **Maintaining the shape** Once the basic shape has been established, it will simply be a matter of trimming two or three times each summer to maintain the precise outline.

SIMPLE BOX SPIRAL
This small box *(Buxus sempervirens)* has been neatly clipped to look as if it is spiraling upward, an effect that is fairly easily achieved.

6

WIRE-TRAINED CLIMBERS

Some climbing plants can also be grown in containers and trained around a wire support to make attractive shapes for the patio or conservatory. Climbers that are suitable for growing in this way include clematis and ivy *(Hedera)* (see also p. 11).

■ **Starting off** Plant the climber in a fairly large container and insert a support into the soil mix. This can be simple in shape, such as a circle, or more elaborate. Tie the shoots loosely into the support as they grow.

■ **Pruning** When the shoots reach the top of the support, you can start to prune back the tips with a pair of pruning shears to accentuate the shape and also to encourage the plant to bush out lower down, and produce flowers (if it is a flowering climber) all around the shape.

WIRE-TRAINED JASMINE
When this jasmine has covered its support and is in full flower, the shape will be more pronounced, and the feature very eye-catching.

PLANTS SUITABLE FOR TOPIARY

Laurus nobilis
Bay
Quick-growing; ideal for bold, yet simple shapes, like a cone or sphere.

Buxus sempervirens
Box
For both intricate and simple shapes.

Cupressus sempervirens
Cypress
Used in ready-made topiary spirals.

Hedera
Ivy
Easily trained on a wire framework.

Ligustrum ovalifolium
Privet
Best for simple shapes. Use golden-leaved 'Aureum' for more impact

Taxus baccata
Yew
Suits complicated geometric shapes.

6

BONSAI

The Japanese technique of bonsai involves the creation of miniature versions of trees such as larch, maple, and pine in small containers. Roots are severely pruned and restricted, and main stems cut back and trained into shape using wires and strings. A successful bonsai needs to look as natural as possible. In order to achieve the necessary dwarf growth habit, the pot must be the right size, the branches, twigs, and roots regularly pruned, and the shoots and buds pinched out.

SHAPING A BONSAI

To establish the basic shape, you will need to prune away any unnecessary branches. Once the desired shape has been formed, remove new growth in good time, not only to maintain the shape and size of tree but also to encourage growth lower down the plant. If new shoots are regularly cut back, the crown of the tree will be much more compact and dense.

INDOOR BONSAI

• Bonsai that have spent the winter months indoors, in fluctuating levels of light and temperature, will often produce an abundance of growth in spring. Wait three or four weeks before attempting any pruning and shaping, to give the tree a chance to spread its branches.

• When a bonsai is brought back indoors at the end of summer, do not be tempted to cut off any sickly looking growth, as this may be the result of changes in light and temperature. It needs time to reacclimatize itself to these different conditions. Any unwanted, healthy new growth can still be removed as and when the need arises.

ROUTINE PRUNING

Bonsai should be pruned in summer. When pruning a bonsai, as with any other plant, the cuts must be as clean as possible, taking care not to leave any stumps behind. The angle of the cut should be made so that water runs away from the bud, otherwise rot, dieback, or disease may result.

The most natural way to shape a tree is to prune to a bud that is facing in the direction in which you would like a new branch to grow. By cutting back to this bud, new growth will be forced in that direction. As summer progresses, growth will slow and the bonsai will need less pruning; pruning should cease altogether by the end of summer.

■ **Pruning conifers** Conifers such as cryptomerias and junipers *(Juniperus)* should have their developing shoots pinched out almost daily to maintain a compact, bushy appearance.

■ **Pruning deciduous trees** Trees such as maples *(Acer)* and zelkovas need their shoots removed or shortened throughout the growing season.

■ **Exceptions to the rule** Cut back beeches *(Fagus)* and Japanese white pines *(Pinus parviflora)* only once, as new growth commences, when their shoots are still soft.

6

ROOT PRUNING

Even though a bonsai tree has its branches pruned drastically, the roots will continue to grow. Rather than moving the bonsai into a larger pot, it is usually better to prune its roots and repot it into the same container.

Root pruning is best carried out in spring. The soil mix should be allowed to dry out somewhat before you carry out root pruning.

■ **How to root prune** Gently remove the bonsai from its pot. Unwind and remove any roots that are winding around the rootball. Tease one-third of the roots away from the rootball, removing as much soil as possible. In the case of evergreens, tease roughly a quarter of the roots free. Cut these off cleanly, using sharp scissors. Replant the bonsai in the same pot.

BONSAI JUNIPER
This juniper *(Juniperus chinensis)* is a fine example of a mature bonsai tree: a miniature version of the full-size tree that is perfectly in proportion.

6

FEATURE PLANTS

Often used in gardens to create a focal point, trained fuchsias and ornamental grasses are two of the most popular feature plants. Fuchsias can be trained as standards, pyramids, or fans, while the architectural form of grasses and bamboos produces a fine display.

STANDARD FUCHSIAS

Find a cutting which has three leaves at a joint instead of two. These will each produce three shoots and so form a bushier head with more flowers. Pot the cutting in a 3-in (8-cm) pot and tie the stem to a cane. As it grows, keep tying it to the cane to keep it straight. Sideshoots will develop from the leaf axils; remove these, but do not remove any leaves. The plant needs to grow without check, so keep repotting it into a pot one size larger. The final pot should be 9in (23cm) deep. When the plant is 1–3ft (30–90cm) tall, pinch out the top of the main stem. Keep pinching out all new shoots as soon as they have three or four leaves to encourage a bushy head. Pinch or remove any shoots that appear on the stem.

A WELL-BALANCED STANDARD
The correct pruning method should result in a sturdy, single-stemmed plant, like this one, supporting a bushy head bearing plenty of flowers.

PYRAMID AND FAN FUCHSIAS

Similar techniques can be employed to train fuchsias as pyramids or fans.

■ **Pyramid** Grow a single-stemmed plant until the main stem is about 30in (75cm) tall. Then pinch out the tip and allow sideshoots to develop. Stop these at two or three pairs of leaves, but let the uppermost shoot grow another 12in (30cm) or so. Then stop this tip, letting more sideshoots grow. Repeat the process until the required height is reached.

■ **Fan** Spread out the shoots and train them in to a framework of canes, pinching out any sideshoots to encourage more shoots to form.

ORNAMENTAL GRASSES

Most ornamental grasses respond to hard pruning in spring, when you should shear the clump right down almost to ground level. This will encourage the plant to produce new growth from the base. Thereafter, trim off discolored foliage and flower heads as they are seen.

■ **Pampas grass** *(Cortaderia selloana)* This is a large, clump-forming grass that is grown for its spectacular, plumelike flower heads.

These are usually left on for winter decoration, but when spring comes around they can look a sorry sight. Use a pair of shears to trim off the dead flower stems and foliage, cutting as near to the ground as possible without damaging any new growth.

Older plants tend to get congested with dead foliage. Pull these old stem bases out from the center of the clump in order to allow new shoots to grow. Always wear thick gloves, as pampas grass leaves are razor sharp.

GARDEN BAMBOOS

Many types of bamboo are suitable for growing in gardens, including the Chilean bamboo *(Chusquea culeou)*. Thin out some of its older canes each spring in order to open up the center of the clump. For other bamboos, you should completely remove any canes that are broken, frost-damaged, or discolored in spring.

■ **Pruning technique** Use loppers to cut the canes, and always wear thick gloves when handling bamboo.

■ **Promoting new growth** With bamboos that are grown for their colored canes or variegated leaves, such as the white-stripe bamboo *(Arundinaria variegata)*, it is a good idea to cut them right back to the ground occasionally in order to encourage the production of healthy new growth from the base.

■ **Thinning bamboo** Whenever a bamboo clump becomes too dense,

a few of the oldest canes can be thinned out, taking them right down to the base. Take care not to damage any new shoots and clear away any debris at the base of the plant to let in light and air.

DECORATIVE SEDGE
The slender stems and dainty flowering spikes of sedges are easily damaged by frosts and wind in fall. Cut them down after flowering to stimulate new growth.

6

HOUSEPLANTS

From time to time, nearly all houseplants will need some kind of pruning, to a greater or lesser degree, usually because they have grown too big for their allotted space. If a plant has grown out of shape or too leggy, you can cut it back using pruning shears or a sharp pair of scissors. Always make any cuts just above a healthy growth bud on the stem. Since pruning facilitates growth, the harder you prune the more new growth you will help to form.

PINCHING OUT OR STOPPING

To encourage a houseplant to curb its natural tendency to throw out long stems and instead produce a compact, bushy plant, you need to employ a certain kind of pruning technique known as pinching out or stopping. Trace leading shoots back to where they grow away from a leaf, and then simply remove them by cutting or pinching them off at that point. This encourages the plant to send out two or more stems from buds a little below this point and, if these are treated in the same way when they are long enough, a bushier plant will result. Most houseplants respond to this treatment, especially foliage plants such as coleus, pileas, tradescantias, and zebrinas.

PINCHING OUT
Removing the tips of leading shoots encourages the houseplant, in this case a coleus, to produce more shoots and leaves lower down the plant.

RESTRICTING TALL-GROWING PLANTS

Once certain climbers and tall-growing indoor plants threaten to reach the roof or ceiling, the time has come to take action, unless you want to have a green canopy over your head. You can try removing their leading shoots, but this operation can only be carried out a couple of times before the lower part of the stem starts to become leafless and woody.

■ **Drastic pruning** Severe pruning is the best course of action with such an overgrown plant, cutting back to

growth buds within 6in (15cm) or so of its base. In time, the plant will throw up a number of shoots from this point. These shoots can then be treated as cuttings and, as soon as they are established, they can be used to replace the old plant.

■ **Suitable plants** Plants that respond well to this include kangaroo vines (*Cissus antarctica*), dieffenbachias, fatsias, umbrella plants (*Schefflera*), grape ivies (*Cissus rhombifolia*), and most ornamental figs (*Ficus*).

PRUNING A RUBBER PLANT

The act of pruning a rubber plant *(Ficus elastica)* can be a challenge, as you have to chop its "head" off. It is a job best done during winter, when the rubber plant is more or less dormant and there is not so much milky sap flowing through its stems to bleed out when they are cut.

1 With sharp pruning shears, cut through the main stem just above a leaf. Leave at least 2ft (60cm) between the top of the plant and the ceiling to allow for new growth.

2 Check the flow of milky sap by applying a little damp soil mix to the cut. When new shoots appear there will be three or more branching ones rather than the single stem there was before. You can cut up the severed section into individual leaves, each with a piece of stem attached, and use these as cuttings.

6

TRAINING AND PRUNING A POT-GROWN JASMINE

The jasmine *Jasminum polyanthum* is a widely grown house- and conservatory plant, its star-shaped white flowers scenting the air from late spring to early summer. It flowers on shoots made in the previous year and, if it is pruned immediately after flowering, it will live to flower another year. This jasmine is usually trained to grow up and around a wire hoop or up a trellis and, although it will stay quite small when confined to a pot, its stems will soon form a congested mass if they are not pruned annually, as shown and described below.

1 Carefully detach all the stems from their support, and gently untangle them.

2 Cut back all the long, flowered shoots to nonflowering sideshoots or a pair of healthy buds.

6

3 Repot or top-dress the plant, and check that the support is still sound.

4 Retrain the plant carefully, tying stems in to the support at even intervals. Apply fertilizer, and train any strong new shoots horizontally to stimulate flowering sideshoots.

PRUNING BOUGAINVILLEA

Bougainvilleas can be trained against a warm conservatory wall where they will flower on the current season's growth from summer to fall. Prune in late winter or early spring, while the plant is dormant. Take care of your eyes when pruning, as the stems have vicious barbs on them.

■ **Formative pruning** Cut back new plants hard, to stimulate new growth from the base. Choose half a dozen strong shoots and shorten them to 6–8in (15–20cm). As the aim is to create a fan shape, cut back to an outward-facing bud. Remove any weak and spindly growth. As new shoots grow, tie them in, in a fan-shaped arrangement.

In the following spring, prune the previous year's growth back by three-quarters. Tie in new shoots as they appear. To promote the development of flowering spurs, cut the sideshoots back to two or three leaves or buds.

Repeat this pruning routine each spring until the plant has covered its allotted space.

■ **Routine pruning** Once the basic permanent framework of the plant has been established, routine pruning is simply a matter of cutting back wayward shoots to a healthy bud or sideshoot early each spring. Shorten the previous season's sideshoots to two or three buds, leaving spurs about 1in (2.5cm) long, from which flowering shoots will form.

In summer, you should remove any dead and damaged stems as necessary, and deadhead by cutting entire flower trusses back to young, nonflowering sideshoots.

6

KITCHEN CROPS

The pruning of edible crops, such as pot-grown fruit trees, herbs, tomatoes, and citrus fruits, is carried out to maximize their cropping potential or to enhance their decorative value. Bay trees can also be pruned to grow as potted standards.

KITCHEN HERBS

To ensure a supply of fresh young foliage, it is a good idea to cut most herbs back hard once or twice in the growing season. Thyme prefers a light pruning only. Vigorous herbs, such as mint, quickly outgrow their allotted space so make sure that you remove runners as they appear.

Not only decorative, a standard bay tree also has culinary uses and, if the weather turns really cold, a potted bay can easily be given the shelter of a frost-free greenhouse or conservatory. It takes a few years to achieve a good, roundheaded standard bay but, with a little

patience, there is no reason why you cannot create one yourself. Choose a plant that has a good, strong main stem. When the plant reaches 2ft (60cm), cut the lowest branches off flush with the main stem. This will encourage growth on the upper branches. When the bay reaches the desired height, stop the leading branch. Each spring and summer, prune back new growth to create and maintain a rounded head.

POT-GROWN TREE FRUITS

Tree fruits need to be grafted onto a dwarfing rootstock if they are to be grown in a container, so that growth and vigor are kept under control. Apples, cherries, and peaches are now often available in this form. The pot should be 12–15in (30–38cm) in diameter and have good drainage.

Prune apples in winter, and cherries and peaches in midspring. After planting, cut the main and other upper branches back to within 6in (15cm) of the main stem, and cut all lower branches back to 10in (25cm), to create the main framework. Take out weak or crossing branches not needed for the framework.

Once established, cut the main stem back to a strong bud each year.

KEPT IN TRIM
Many small container-grown herbs, such as basil, are kept in trim through regular harvesting of their leaves.

6

GREENHOUSE
TOMATOES
Tomatoes crop best
when encouraged to
grow upward rather
than bush out
sideways. This entails
gently pinching out
the sideshoots.

Alternate the side on which this bud is located, so the stem will keep growing straight up. Cut back new growth to within 6in (15cm) of the old growth, and remove damaged or weak growth. A light summer prune will help maintain an upright shape.

Most citrus fruits can bear fruit even in cool climates, where they are best grown as a potted standard in a sunny spot in summer and brought under cover during the winter. Prune young trees from spring until late summer, and established trees after harvesting fruit.

Lightly stake the young tree, then reduce sideshoots by one-third. When it has reached the desired height, cut the leader back to a strong bud. Retain four, well-spaced shoots to form the head, removing three or four leaves from each. Remove all other sideshoots and any regrowth on the stem. Once established, remove the stake. Routine pruning consists of cutting fruited shoots back to a nonfruiting sideshoot and removing the growing tips of shoots on main branches.

PRUNING TOMATOES

Tomatoes grown both outdoors and under glass need pinch pruning to keep them growing upward and able to carry more fruit. Sideshoots are produced in the leaf axils (between the leaf stalks and the main stem) and should be removed as soon as they are seen. Use your thumb and finger or a pair of nail scissors, taking care not to damage the fruit clusters. They will also need stopping, so that they do not produce more fruit than they can cope with. On outdoor plants, remove the growing tip once four or five flower clusters have formed. Under cover, half a dozen clusters can be allowed to set on each plant before it needs to be stopped.

6

INDEX

Apples 74–75
Apricots 83
Arbors 62
Arches 62
Bamboos 105
Bay trees 110
Blackberries 91
Black currants 88
Blueberries 91
Bonsai 11, 102–103
Boston ivy 67
Bougainvillea 109
Buds
  alternate 16
  opposite 16
Cherries 84
Citrus fruits 111
Clematis 64–65
Cordons 78, 93
Deadheading 55
Espaliers 80
Fan-training 83, 84–85
Feeding 17
Figs 86
Fruit
  thinning 94
  trees 73, 110
Fuchsias 104
Gooseberries 89
Grapevines 92–93, 94
Grasses 105

Guyot system 92
Hedges 36–37
Herbs 110
Honeysuckle 66–67
Houseplants 107
Ivy 69
Jasmine 68, 108
Laburnum 97
Loganberries 91
Mildew 89
Mulberries 87
Mulching 17
Nectarines 83
Obelisks 98
Peaches 83
Pears 74–75
Pergolas 62
Pinching out 106
Pleaching 43
Plums 83
Pollarding 42
Pruning
  cuts 16–17
  hard 16
  moderate 16
  light 16
  terms 20–22
  tools 18–19
Quinces 87
Raspberries 90
Red currants 89
Root pruning 42
Roses 46–47, 98–99
  climbing 49–50

ground-cover 52
miniature 53
Modern bush 48
modern shrub 51
old garden 51
rambling 49–50
standard 52
Rubber plant 107
Russian vine 67
Screens 62
Seasonal tasks 14–15, 56
Shoots
  reverted 8
  water 9
Shrubs 12, 24–25
  colored-stemmed 31
  container 32–33
  early flowering 26–27
  evergreens 29–30
  gray-leaved 29–30
  late-flowering 28–29
  small-leaved 31
  wall-trained 34–35
Silver leaf disease 82

Soft fruits 72–73
Standards 104, 110
Strawberries 91
Suckers 9, 54, 82
Supports 61
Swags 99
Tomatoes 111
Toolcare 19
Topiary 11, 100–101
Training 10, 34, 59, 61, 96–97
Trees 40–41
  deciduous 12, 102
  evergreens 13, 44, 102
  pot-grown 110
  preservation 43
  spur-bearing 77
  tip-bearing 77
Trellises 62
Tripods 98
Virginia creeper 67
Walls 62, 70
Wire-training 62, 101
White currants 89
Wisteria 67, 97
Worcesterberries 91
Wounds 24

ACKNOWLEDGMENTS

p. 9 Jerry Harpur/designer Helen Yemem; p. 15 Jerry Harpur/designer Lisette Pleasance, London; p. 16 Steven Wooster/designer Geoffrey Whiten; p. 19 Jerry Harpur/designer Isabelle Green, California; p. 21 Steven Wooster/designer Terence Conran; p. 24 Andrew Lawson/designer Anthony Noel; p. 30 Steven Wooster/designer Carol Klein; p. 31 Steven Wooster/designer Terence Conran; p. 33 Steven Wooster/designer Carol Klein; p. 34 John Glover; p. 36, p. 37 Steven Wooster/deisgner Terence Conran; p. 39 Steven Wooster/designer Chris Gregory; p. 57 Jerry Harpur/designer Anne Alexander-Sinclair; p. 58 Andrew Lawson; p. 63 Jerry Harpur/designer Edwina von Gal, New York City; p. 70 Andrew Lawson; p. 72 Steven Wooster/Fairweather Sculpture; p. 76 Steven Wooster/designer Carol Klein; p. 92 Marcus Harpur/designer Susan Rowley; p. 93 Marcus Harpur/designer Susan Rowley; p. 107 John Glover; p. 108 John Glover. Thanks to Tim Stansfield; Country Gardens, Tring; Jane Haley-Pursey and staff at Solesbridge Mill Water Gardens, Chorleywood; and Spear and Jackson.

can record them! You are awesome! Love, Grandmother 10/14/18

THIS TRAVEL JOURNAL BELONGS TO

_____

VACATION TITLE

_____

TRIP DATES

_____ / _____ / _____ to _____ / _____ / _____

I dedicate this Inspired Vacation Journal to

_____

because _____

_____

the inspired
VACATION
JOURNAL

created by Kim LaCroix
designed by Works Progress Design

Dear Parents,

Have you ever wondered what it takes to transform a moment into a lasting and cherished memory?

One night, as I washed my daughter's hair, it struck me. A memory flooded back of my mom styling my foamy hair into a unicorn horn. So, at that very moment, I styled my daughter's hair the same way. We shared a giddy laugh, and we planted the seed of a cherished memory.

Parenting today is harder than ever. We live as parents driven by a desire to create these moments with our kids, but are constrained by everything else. We are in competition with sports, work, homework, video games, and the TV remote.

Imagine what it would be like to know that you're living life alongside your kids the way you know it should be lived—where quality time isn't just an afterthought, but something you're able to create purposefully with your whole family.

From more than a decade of experience in the field of education, I created **The Inspired Vacation Journal** to help us find our own "unicorn moments," while helping kids practice a critical life skill: writing.

This travel journal gives your child structured and meaningful writing prompts to engage their senses. But it's far more than that—it's designed to help you connect with and enrich your kiddos, and savor those memories for years to come. And, it's powered by fun, so they'll happily participate.

Who knows? Maybe this journal can help you find some guiltless quiet vacation time of your own.

Kim LaCroix

Kim LaCroix
Mother of two, author of **The Inspired Vacation Journal**

How to use *The Inspired Vacation Journal*

Because this journal is an authentic writing experience, your child will write with a genuine purpose, and for a genuine audience. With journals, much like memos and to-do lists, the writer also becomes the reader, but this journal isn't a personal diary, rather it's meant to be shared.

The ONLY caveat to sharing is that there is no room for expectations or criticism on this journey. The end result won't be red pen markings, and a teacher will not be the ultimate audience. This is an opportunity for your child to write about a special time, and remember it for years to come, immortalized in his or her own words. It's an opportunity for you to say, "Wow, look what you did!"

There's no need nag your child to "do" this journal, but bring it along to the restaurant, just in case. You might even find some time for adult conversation, or maybe it'll stimulate some seriously fun family talk.

The materials needed for **The Inspired Vacation Journal** can be found around the house, or you can bring along The Inspired Pencil Pack, which includes the following:

- **Colored pencils/pencils**
- **Highlighters**
- **Tape or glue**
- **Scissors**
- **Sticky notes**

And, don't forget to save your remnants in the folder in the back of the book, little things that remind you of BIG times (ticket stubs, maps, mementos...any little thing can be a remnant).

Above all else, have fun out there! And, when you get home, bring out the journal every so often. You'll be amazed by what happens!

Info for parents:

PRIZE PAGE INSTRUCTIONS:

➤ Pick a reward from the reward sticker set (or draw your own).

➤ Choose where to to place it on the prize grid. For example, in the grid below, the ice cream prize sticker is in the 4th block which means the writer needs to finish 4 journal entries before going out for ice cream. After 5 more, it's movie time!

➤ Mark a check for each journal activity completed.

➤ Don't wait to give your child his/her reward! The prize should come soon after earning it.

➤ Please explain the reward system to your young writer.

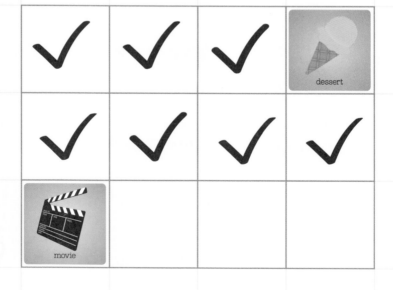

PRIZE PAGE!

Each box represents the completion
of one journal activity.

1	2	3	4
5	6	7	8
9	10	11	12
13	14	15	16
17	18	19	20
21	22	23	24

DON'T FORGET TO WRITE!

Write a few (that's 3) of your **favorite** people's addresses below so you can send them postcards.

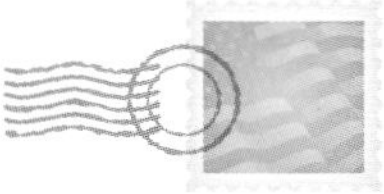

Miss you!

_____
name

_____
street address

_____
city, state, zip code, country

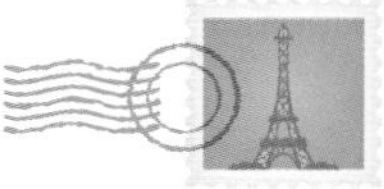

Having fun in _____

_____
name

_____
street address

_____
city, state, zip code, country

See you soon!

_____
name

_____
street address

_____
city, state, zip code, country

AUTOGRAPHS

Collect autographs of friends you meet along the way!

I wish I could get a signature from _____

_____

because _____

_____

Penn was here!

Circle all the ways you traveled on your vacation!

GETTING AROUND

Draw another here!

I've always wanted to travel by _____

because _____

_____

☐ I did it!

☐ I still want to do it.

MAP IT

Circle your country or state. Color the places you visit with your favorite colors!

Greenland

Alaska

Nunavut

Yukon
Territory

Northwest
Territories

Canada

British
Columbia

Alberta

Saskatchewan

Manitoba

Ontario

Quebec

Newfoundland
&
Labrador

Ireland

Nova
Scotia

United States

Mexico

*North
Pacific
Ocean*

*North
Atlantic
Ocean*

Azores

Portugal

Canary Islands

Western Sahara
(Occupied by Morocco)

Cape Verde

Bahamas

Cuba

Dom. Rep.

Jamaica

Haiti

Puerto Rico
S. Kitts & Nevis

Antigua & Barbuda

Dominica

St. Lucia
Barbados

St. Vincent & the Grenadines

Grenada

Trinidad & Tobago

Belize

Guatemala

Honduras

El Salvador

Nicaragua

Panama

Costa Rica

Venezuela

Colombia

Guyana

Ecuador

Peru

Brazil

Bolivia

Paraguay

Chile

Uruguay

Argentina

*Sou
Atlan
Oce*

Falkland Islands

South Georgia

Tierra Del Fuego

South Pacific Ocean

I live in

_____
state or country

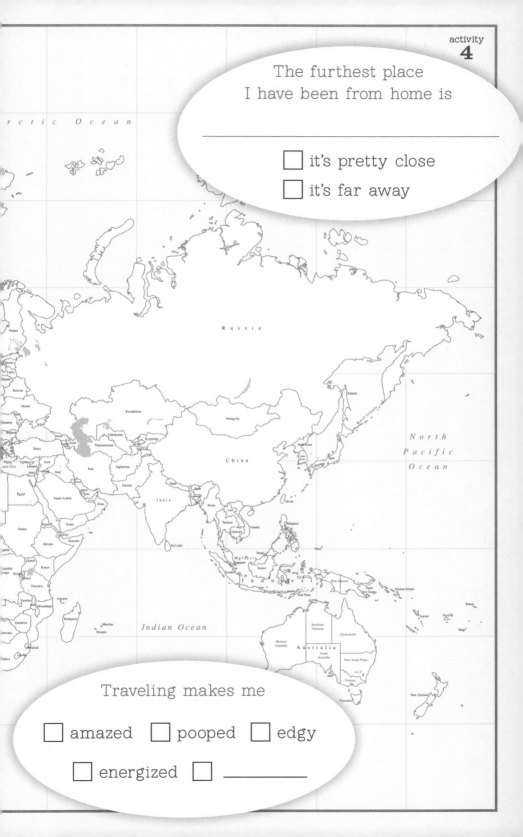

The furthest place
I have been from home is

_____

☐ it's pretty close
☐ it's far away

Traveling makes me

☐ amazed ☐ pooped ☐ edgy

☐ energized ☐ _____

heads or

Flip a coin! If it's **heads** write...

the **supersilliest** thing

that happened today...

_____

_____

_____

If it's **tails** write...

Today I **wished**... _____

_____

_____

One thing I **thought** about today was...

_____

Today I am **thankful** for...

_____

_____

Don't have a coin? Ask an adult. You might just get to keep it!

CUBE WRITING!

step

Put the cube together.

1. Cut along the blue line to remove the page.

2. Cut on the solid black lines.

3. Fold on the dotted lines.

4. Glue or tape the yellow flaps to the panel with the matching letters.

step

Roll the cube!

Whatever you roll is what you write about on the following page.

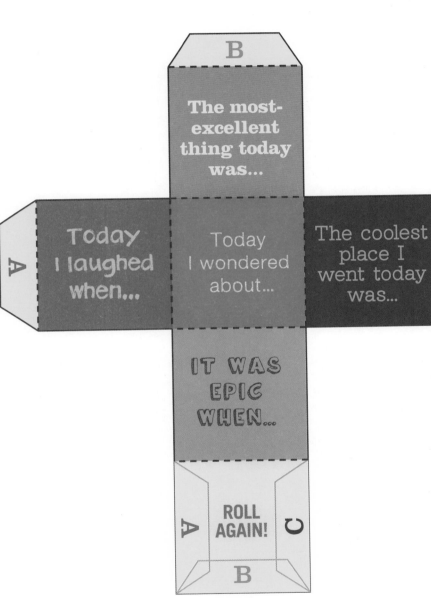

B

The most-excellent thing today was...

A

Today I laughed when...

Today I wondered about...

The coolest place I went today was...

C

IT WAS EPIC WHEN...

A ROLL AGAIN! **C**

B

ROLL THE CUBE!

Highlight the cube side you rolled and then answer.

Today I laughed when...

The most-excellent thing today was...

The coolest place I went today was...

Today I wondered about...

IT WAS EPIC WHEN...

Start writing here.

_____

_____

because _____

_____

my colossal idea today

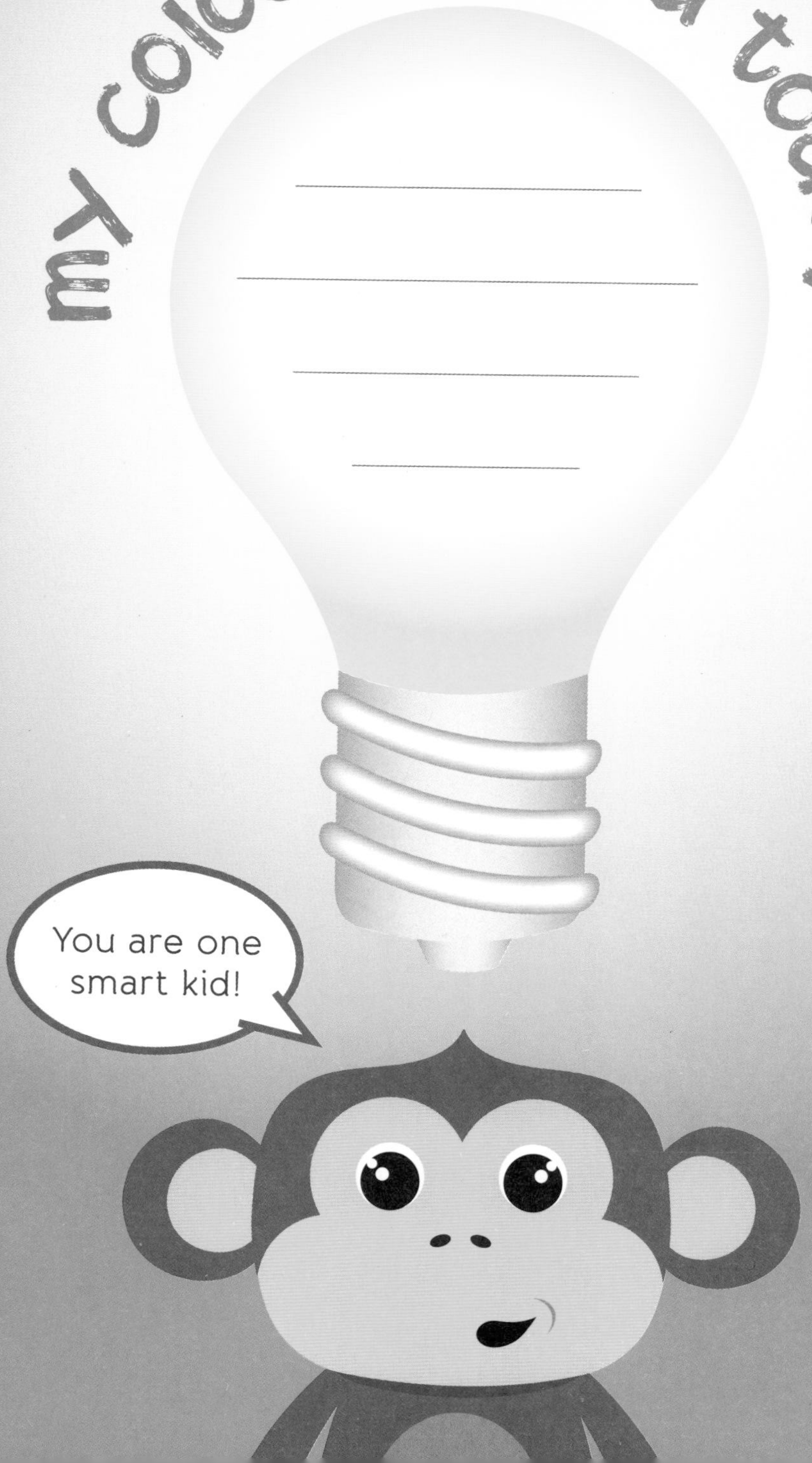

STICK AROUND!

Use 3 different sticky
notes to write or
draw some things
describing your trip
so far. Stick them
anywhere you
want on this page.

sketch artist!

Bring your journal along and draw.

Let me tell you about my drawing. _____

_____

_____

_____

My picture looks... ☐ kind of like it

☐ just like it

☐ nothing like it

CHAIN OF EVENTS

Draw and write about 3 things
that happened today!

1st

2nd

3rd

highlight of the day

the **YIPPEE!**

I wanted to cheer **"YIPPEE!"** when _____

_____

_____

_____

_____

& the **YUCKY!**

I wanted to shout **"YUCKY!"** when _____

_____

_____

_____

_____

bummer!

remnant writing

Remnants are **small** things reminding you of **BIG** times! Glue or tape a remnant you've saved in the back pocket here.

I chose to use this **remnant** because I want to **REMEMBER**

_____

_____

_____

restaurant review

Tell them what you think by writing a review!

Dear _____,
restaurant name

I visited your restaurant on _____.
date (for example: July 10, 2012)

_____ was the name of my server.
name of your waiter or waitress

I thought you might like to hear my thoughts about my visit

to your restaurant. Thanks for listening!

rating key:

☆ = pretty unacceptable

☆☆ = somewhat inspiring

☆☆☆ = liked it

☆☆☆☆ = loved it

☆☆☆☆☆ = fabulous!

Sincerely,

_____
your name

Highlight the stars below to show your review.

☆☆☆☆☆ yummy factor

☆☆☆☆☆ kid-friendliness

☆☆☆☆☆ service

☆☆☆☆☆ fun-factor

☆☆☆☆☆ overall rating

Additional comments:

↙

_____

_____

hi there!

I'm Penn. This review is an activity from *The Inspired Vacation Journal*—a kid's travel journal that encourages the love of writing. By accepting this review, you're helping this child learn that his/her thoughts and ideas matter in the world. If you want to learn more, visit **inspiredpencil.com**. Thanks for your support!

xoxo,
PENN

REPORTER'S NOTEBOOK

Ask your parent, brother, sister, cousin, or friend
if you can interview them. Don't forget to say
"please" and "thank you"!

This is my interview with:

Question #1: What are you thankful for today?

Question #2: Tell me one spectacular memory
about our trip.

Question #3: What's one thing you thought
about today?

Question #4: (Make up your own question!)

something OLD

The OLDEST thing I've seen is: _____

_____

Let me tell you about it: _____

_____

_____

This is what it looks like!

something NEW

The **NEWEST** thing I've seen is: _____

_____

Let me tell you about it: _____

_____

_____

This is what it looks like!

spira-list

Write on the spiral line...

Today I saw...

flip flop

List some of the incredible things you did
then flip the page and draw one.

On my vacation I...

_____

_____

_____

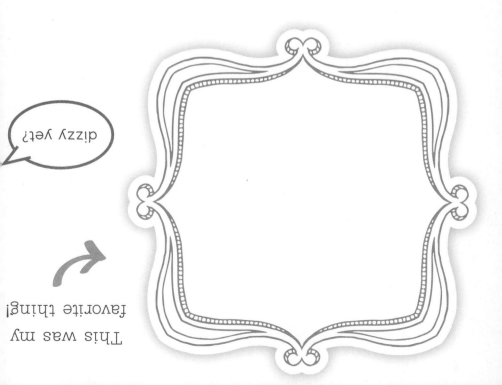

dizzy yet?

This was my
favorite thing!

BEST OF...

kids' pick

You get to choose!

The **BEST** activity: _____

_____

The **YUMMIEST** food: _____

_____

The **MOST COMFY** home away from home:

_____

The **FIRST THING** I want to do when I get home is:

_____

_____

BEST OF...

adults'
pick

Ask an adult!
Write his/her name here:

_____

The **BEST** activity: _____

_____

The **YUMMIEST** food: _____

_____

The **MOST COMFY** home away from home:

_____

Same as me: ☐

Different than me: ☐

REMEMBER WHEN...

DRAW a picture of the thing you'll remember most. Then **WRITE** about it!

_____

_____

_____

journal review &
race to get home!

Please review your journal experience by
filling this out and mailing it to me!
The moment it arrives in my mailbox, I will
record it on my website on the **Race to Get Home**
page. Wonder who will get home first, you or your
letter to me? You might even win one of our
monthly prizes—check the website for the
current Inspired Pencil contest!

Your friend,

Penn

_____   _____
first name   your email (optional)

Where I went: _____

Highlight the stars below to show your review.

☆☆☆☆☆ fun-factor (I loved writing in my journal!)
☆☆☆☆☆ inspiration (I want to write more!)
☆☆☆☆☆ recommendation (I'd give one to a friend!)
☆☆☆☆☆ parent's review
☆☆☆☆☆ overall rating

Most favorite page: _____

Least favorite page: _____

Just thought I'd tell you... _____

▼ fold here ▼

2307 Oak Street
Virginia Beach, VA 23451

place
stamp
here

The Inspired Pencil
2307 Oak Street
Virginia Beach, VA 23451

▲ fold here ▲

Parents and kids:

Please visit us at **inspiredpencil.com**!
We'll gladly accept your review or
comments there as well.

glue goes here

sketch pages

The rest of these pages are just for you.
Draw, play games, sketch, journal...anything you wish!